South Africa:
The Land, Its People and History

Willie Seth

Copyright (c) 2008 Willie Seth
All rights reserved.

South Africa: The Land, Its People and History
Willie Seth

First Edition

ISBN 978-0-9802587-5-8

No part of this book may be reproduced in any form for commercial purposes without written permission from the publisher.

New Africa Press
Pretoria, South Africa

Dedication

To the youth of Africa
and future generations

Contents

Acknowledgements

Introduction

Part I:

Historical Background: Birth and Growth of A Nation

Part II:

The Land

Part III:

The People

Part IV:

Black African Immigrants

Acknowledgements

I WISH to express my profound gratitude to all the sources I have cited in this book. They are mentioned throughout the text with full attribution.

And the ones I may have inadvertently omitted where they are supposed to be acknowledged in the book are mentioned elsewhere in my work as indispensable citations.

Special thanks must go to four South African newspapers, the *Mail&Guardian*, the *Sowetan*, *The Times*, and the *Independent* which served as a vital source of information on the xenophobic violence that rocked the nation in May 2008.

I am also indebted to BBC and other sources on the same subject.

The attacks were launched by black South Africans to drive black African immigrants out of the country.

I would not have been able to write the chapter on the subject, the way I did, without the information I obtained from the sources I have mentioned here. And I will always be grateful to them for that.

I am also very thankful to the South African

newspapers I have mentioned, and to BBC, for some of their material I have incorporated into my work and which constitute a substantial part of the appendix on the xenophobic terror I have compiled to address one of the most important events in the history of South Africa since the end of apartheid.

It was the worst form of violence since the end of white minority rule in that country and it tarnished the image of South Africa as a rainbow nation, if it ever indeed was one.

One book also deserves special mention. It had a profound impact on the conception and execution of this project in many fundamental respects. And that is *South Africa in Contemporary Times* by Tanzanian writer Godfrey Mwakikagile.

It inspired me in many ways and influenced the course of my work in a way I never expected it would.

And I highly recommend it to anyone who wants to get a good understanding of South Africa in modern times, especially since the seventies and after the end of apartheid. It also addresses some of the most controversial subjects in South Africa in the post-apartheid era.

Anyone who reads my work should also read the other book. They are complementary texts, literary "twins" in some respects, although they also address different subjects.

Writing a book of this nature and magnitude is a collective enterprise. As human beings, we follow paths illuminated by others. Without trail blazers who went before us, we wouldn't be where we are today in terms of knowledge accumulated through the ages and as members of the human race. It is a treasure trove we share, and we are able to see far only because we stand on the shoulders of others.

So, while I am tempted to assume full responsibility for all the mistakes in my work, I can not do so because I am fully aware that I am not the original source of all the information contained in this book.

Others deserve credit for a lot of that, together with the mistakes they may have made in the execution of their projects in pursuit of knowledge accumulated to share with the rest of mankind.

Therefore it is a collective responsibility, although they deserve more credit than I do in the completion of my work. I would not have been able to write this book without them as a source of invaluable information.

But the analysis is mine, and I bear full responsibility for that, also being fully aware that it may be faulty here and there because we are all mere mortals with frailties.

Introduction

THIS IS a general introduction to South Africa, the continent's powerhouse.

South Africa is the most industrialised and most powerful country on the African continent. It is also the richest.

South Africa also is a country that witnessed a miracle – a peaceful transition from one of the most racist and most repressive regimes in history under the diabolical institution of apartheid to a democratic government under which members of all races have equal rights under the law.

But the focus of this study is not on what has taken place in South Africa since the end of apartheid, although we may take a glimpse of that here and there as we go along.

The focus is on the country itself in general: its geography, its people, and its history since its founding more than 300 years ago as a nation composed of different races and ethnic groups, including Dutch settlers and other Europeans who, although a minority, played the most important role in shaping the destiny of South Africa as a racist society dominated by whites until the end of apartheid only a few years ago.

Apartheid ended in the early 1990s only as a political institution. As an economic phenomenon, it still exists in all its manifestations including brutal treatment of black farm workers by their white masters. The economy is still dominated by whites and probably will be for many years to come. But that is an entirely different subject beyond the scope of this work which focuses on South Africa in general.

So, we are going to look at what constitutes South Africa as a nation – the different racial and ethnic groups. We are also going to look at the provinces from a historical and geographical perspective and the people who live in those provinces.

We are also going to look at the country from other perspectives, including South Africa in contemporary times, to get a comprehensive picture of what is unquestionably the most dynamic, and most influential, country on the African continent and which will continue to play a major role in continental affairs for many years to come.

Also addressed in the book is the subject of xenophobic terror against black African immigrants in South Africa.

It constitutes a substantial portion of the book and may have taken a disproportionately large amount of space in this work. But that is for obvious reasons.

It is a very important subject which needs all the attention it can get form those who want to address it. For, the existence of such a phenomenon undermines the very foundations upon which the new South Africa is being built. And if it continues, there will be no South Africa as we know it.

It is going to be an entirely different country, if it is going to exist at all as a functional entity and not become an empty shell reminiscent of Zaire under Mobutu or any of the other African states which have collapsed through the decades, earning Africa the dubious and unenviable distinction as a continent of failed states.

Because of the urgency of the situation, it is imperative that the matter should be addressed accordingly and as comprehensively as possible.

One can never say too much about violence. Silence is a partner of evil and is tantamount to condoning the very evil we want to condemn and eliminate.

Many African countries have descended into chaos, and some of them have dissolved in anarchy, because not enough was done to avert this catastrophe.

South Africa has not reached that point. But if nothing or if not enough is done to neutralise xenophobic violence, failure to do so will inevitably lead to chaos. And it will be an invitation to a reign of terror, earning South Africa the distinction of being – just another African state.

The xenophobic violence is inextricably linked with deprivation and poverty among black South Africans trapped in the townships which are cesspools of diabolical iniquities. There are many good people in the townships. But there also large numbers who are prone to crime and don't value human life.

The failure of the government to address the plight of these people is directly responsible for the explosion which rocked the townships and other parts of South Africa in a wave of xenophobic terror directed against black African immigrants in their midst.

Their plight does not justify violence against the immigrants. But there is no question that it breeds insecurity which in turn is fuelled by poverty. It is a vicious cycle.

It was a catastrophe waiting to happen. Compounding the felony is the fact that the ruling African National Congress (ANC) was, for years, fully aware of this. The leaders knew resentment was brewing and building up in the townships. They knew there was frustration not only among the young but also among those of the older generation for having been left behind after apartheid ended. They saw the fruits of freedom being enjoyed by a relatively few amongst them. Yet the leaders did nothing.

If the xenophobic violence jolts the conscience of the South African leadership into doing something to improve th condition of the masses, and protect the immigrants as well, something good will have come out of it, although whatever good comes out of it is not worthy the destruction that ensued when angry mobs of black South Africans attacked, maimed and killed black African immigrants and destroyed their property in an orgy of violence on an unprecedented scale since the end of apartheid.

And it is a matter that has to be addressed, fully, by all South Africans. If it's ignored, it will continue to be a national crisis.

While I concede that I may have given what some people may consider to be undue prominence to this subject in my book, there's no question that my focus on the subject was dictated by the inescapable fact that you can not begin to understand South Africa in its entirety in contemporary times without looking at what is unquestionably one of the nation's most prominent features as a society. And that is violence.

South Africa is one of the most violent societies in the world. The xenophobic terror I have focused on in the last chapter of this book is only one aspect of this disturbing phenomenon.

And South Africa as a nation can do better than that. So can the rest of Africa.

Part I:

Historical Background: Birth and Growth of A Nation

SOUTH AFRICA was not a vast empty space when white settlers first arrived in that part of the continent. The conflicts they had with the indigenous people are enough evidence showing that wasn't the case.

The region which later became the country of South Africa was already inhabited by so-called Bushmen, so-called Hottentots, and different Bantu ethnic groups from the north when white settlement began in 1652.

In 1488, Portuguese explorer Bartolomeu Dias became the first European to reach the Cape of Good Hope. And the first European settlement was established at the cape by the Dutch East India Company. The colony at the cape later became Cape Town.

The Dutch settlers were soon joined by French and German settlers. These early arrivals came to be known as Boers. And the language which evolved among them through the years came to be known as Afrikaans. It was essentially Dutch, as it still is today, since the Dutch were the dominant group among the settlers.

The people who are called Bushmen have their own African name. They call themselves San and are among the oldest inhabitants of South Africa. Others are the pastoral Khoikhoi whom Europeans renamed Hottentots. The Khoikhoi settled mainly in the southeastern coastal region of South Africa about 2,000 years ago.

Around 700s A.D., other Africans had settled in the northern part of what is South Africa today. They were members of different Bantu ethnic groups who had moved southward from East-Central Africa and spoke related languages.

That is why they came to be known as Bantu. It is a linguistic term and simply means "people" in most of the languages spoken by the members of these ethnic groups. There is no Bantu race.

Let's take Kiswahili or Swahili, the most widely spoken African language – in terms of the numbers of countries which use it – as an example. In Kiswahili, *mtu* means person, and *watu* means people or persons.

And in Kinyakyusa or Nyakyusa, a language spoken by more than one million people who constitute one of the largest ethnic groups in Tanzania (there are also hundreds of thousands of Nyakyusa people in Malawi who are also called Ngonde or Bangonde), *mundu* means person, and *abandu* or *bandu* means people; a term very close to *Bantu*. Terms similar to that are found in other Bantu languages.

And there are many other similarities. The terms *lenja ifile* which gained notoriety in May 2008 when they were uttered by some black South Africans who burned two Mozambicans alive – one miraculously survived while the other one died - immediately come to mind as one of those examples.

The Zulu and other black South Africans say *lenja ifile*,

meaning the dog is dead.

The Nyakyusa of Tanzania and Malawi, in the Nyakyusa language which I spoke in Tanzania for many years as I did Swahili, would say *imbwa jifwile*, which means the same thing as *lenja ifile*: the dog is dead. In Swahili, the same expression is slightly different, *mbwa amekufa*, the dog is dead.

Thus you have a language in East Africa, Nyakyusa, which has striking similarities to a language or languages spoken by black South Africans. And so do many others, and vice versa.

There are many other similarities. For example, the Zulu say *amandhla*, which means power. The Nyakyusa say *amaka*, which also means power. The emphasis in Nyakyusa, as in Zulu, is on the second syllable.

The Zulu, the Ndebele and the Xhosa also say *amanza*, meaning water. The Nyakyusa say *amisi* – emphasis on the second syllable - which means water in Nyakyusa language.

Another example: the Zulu say *ngiphuma*, meaning "I'm from"; the Nyakyusa say *ngufuma*, which also means, "I'm from."

And the language of the Nyakyusa people is called *ikiNyakyusa*. That's what the Nyakyusa call their language, while the Zulu call theirs *isiZulu*, the Ndebele call their language *isiNdebele*, the Xhosa call theirs *isiXhosa* as do other black South Africans who also use the prefix *isi-* in their tribal languages.

And what are the people themselves called in their own languages?

The Nyakyusa are known as *abaNyakyusa* or simply *baNyakyusa* depending on the context in which either of those terms is used. Now look at the similarities.

The Zulu are *amaZulu*, the Xhosa are *amaXhosa*, not very different from *abaNyakyusa*.

And in Nyakyusa language, the Zulu are *abaZulu*, the Xhosa are *abaXhosa*, the Ndebele – *abaNdebele*, and the

Swazi – *abaSwasi*, to give only a few examples.

There's no letter "z" in Nyakyusa language; it's replaced by "s." Also in Nyakyusa language, there's no letter "q." And "r" is replaced by the letter "l," "v" is replaced by "f," and "w" by "b" and other letters in different contexts. For example, *watu wengi* is Swahili meaning "many people." And *wimbo*, which means "song" in Swahili, is *lwimbo* in Nyakyusa. But the plural term, *nyimbo*, which means "songs," is the same in both languages. In Swahili "songs" is *nyimbo*, and in Nyakyusa "songs" is also *nyimbo*.

Also, among the Nyakyusa, the word for father is *tata*. In Southern Sotho, a language spoken by millions of people in South Africa and which is also the most widely spoken language in the country of Lesotho, the word for father is *ntate*; very little difference between the two – *tata* and *ntate*.

The Nyakyusa also say *batata*, a plural term, which means parents or ancestors depending on the context in which the term is used and exclusively for males. For example, *batata bitu* in Nyakyusa means "our parents" (male parents) or "our ancestors" (male ancestors); *batata bosa* means "all our parents or ancestors," while *abasukulu* means "grandparents," male and female.

And *abasukulu bitu* means "our grandparents" in Nyakyusa.

Mother is *juba* in Nyakyusa, and *bajuba* is the plural term meaning "mothers," while *bajuba bitu* means "our mothers."

Nkasi gwangu means "my wife" and *ndume gwangu* means "my husband" in Nyakyusa. *Abakasi bitu* or *bakasi bitu* means "our wives," and *abalume bitu* or *balume bitu* means "our husbands." And *abana bitu* or *bana bitu* means "our children," while *mwana gwangu* means "my child."

Abana bangu or *bana bangu* means "my children."

Mwipwa gwangu means "my uncle" and *abipwa bitu*

means "our uncles" in Nyakyusa.

Also in Kinyakyusa, a*bakamu bitu* means "our relatives," and *abakamu bangu* means "my relatives."

Ingamu jangu means "my name is..." in Nyakyusa, not very much different from Xhosa and Zulu.

The Xhosa and the Zulu say, *igama lam ngu* - "my name is...."

Ingamu jako gwe jwani? means "what's your name?" in Nyakyusa. In Xhosa, it's *Ungubani Igama lakho?* And in Zulu it's *Igama lakho ngubani?* Meaning the same thing, "what's your name?"

Nangisya injila means "show me the way" in Nyakyusa. In Xhosa, it's *Ungandikhombisa indlela.*

While *injila* means "way," in Nyakyusa, it's *indlela* in Xhosa. Very little difference between the two terms.

Even the other two terms, *nangisya* and *Ungandikhombisa,* both of which mean "show me" in Nyakyusa and Xhosa, respectively, sound similar.

In Nyakyusa, *ilopa* means "blood." And *ilopa lyangu* means "my blood." But it means more than just the blood that flows in your veins – it also means "my relative" or "my relatives"; for example, when the Nyakyusa say *bosa aba ba ilopa lyangu,* which means "all of these are of my blood."

And *abandu bitu,* or *bandu bitu,* depending on the context in which *abandu or bandu* is used, means "our people" in Nyakyusa language.

Abatitu means "blacks" in Nyakyusa, while *twe batitu* means "we blacks." *Tuli batitu* means "we are black."

Uswe means "us" in Nyakyusa, and *umwe* means "you" in plural form. It can also be used in this context: *Uswe twe baNyakyusa,* a complete sentence meaning "We Nyakyusa."

Umwe mwe baXhosa means "you Xhosa" in Nyakyusa language.

And *abo* means "those" - for example when the Nyakyusa say *abandu abo* – means "those people," and *abandu aba* means "these people."

AbaSulu aba or *aba abaSulu* means "these Zulu."

AbaNdebele abo or *abo abaNdebele* means "those Ndebele" in Nyakyusa.

There are more than one million Nyakyusa in Tanzania alone and they are one of the largest ethnic groups or tribes out of 126 in the whole country.

And although there are a lot of similarities between Swahili and other African languages, from which Swahili itself evolved adding Arabic and other foreign words to it, there are still some differences.

For example, "road" in Kiswahili is *barabara*. In Nyakyusa, or Kinyakyusa, the word for "road" is *nsebo*, and for "roads" is *misebo*.

In Swahili, the plural form is the same – *barabara*, meaning "roads" just as it means "road."

Chakula means "food" in Swahili or Kiswahili. In Nyakyusa or Kinyakyusa, food is *findu* or *ifindu*.

Mto means "river" in Swahili; it also means "pillow." In Nyakyusa language, a river is called *lwisi* or *ulwisi*.

Ifilombe or *filombe* means "maize" in Nyakyusa. In Swahili, "maize" is *mahindi*.

Unga means "flour" in Swahili. In Nyakyusa, "flour" is *ubufu* or *bufu*.

Indima or *ndima* means "beans" in Nyakyusa. In Swahili, "beans" is *maharagwe*.

The word for "lion" in Swahili is *simba*; in Nyakyusa it's *ingalamu* or *ngalamu*.

Mamba means "crocodile" in Swahili. In Nyakyusa, "crocodile" is *ngwina* or *ingwina*.

Swahili for elephant is *tembo*; Nyakyusa – *sofu* or *isofu*.

Swahili for "python" - *chatu*; Nyakyusa – *sota* or *isota*.

But there are some similarities also. Another word for "elephant" in Swahili is *ndovu*, clearly derived from Bantu languages and close to the Nyakyusa word *sofu* for "elephant" but even much closer to those of other Bantu languages.

For example, the Zulu say *ndlovu*, meaning "elephant"; the Venda of South Africa and southern Zimbabwe say *ndou*, also meaning "elephant."

The Venda also say *thoho ya ndou*, meaning "head of an elephant." In Swahili it's *kichwa cha ndovu*, and in Nyakyusa, *untwa gwa sofu*.

In Bemba, spoken in Zambia, *mutwe ulekalipa* means "my head is painful" or "I have a headache." The term *mutwe* for "head" is close to the Nyakyusa term *untwa* or *ntwa* and to the Swahili term *kichwa* all of which mean "head."

The word for "drum" in Venda is *ngoma*. Also in Swahili, *ngoma* means "drum" or "drums".

The Nyakyusa have a completely different word for that. *Ndingala, or indingala* means "drum." Either one can also be used to mean "drums" in Nyakyusa depending on the context in which the term is used.

In Nyakyusa, or ikiNyakyusa as the Nyakyusa call their language, a*balindwana* means "girls." In Swahili, the word for "girls" is *wasichana*, which is completely different from the Nyakyusa word *abalindwana* for "girls."

Ilumbu gwako means "your sister" in Kinyakyusa or Nyakyusa. In Kiswahili or Swahili, *dada yako* means "your sister."

Nkasi means "wife" in Nyakyusa. In Swahili, "wife" is *mke*.

Nkasi gwangu or *unkasi gwangu*, depending on the context, means "my wife" in Nyakyusa. In Swahili, "my wife" is *mke wangu*.

Mguu means "leg" and *miguu* means "legs" in Swahili. In Nyakyusa, the word for "leg" is *kilundi*, and for "legs" - *filundi*.

Mguu wangu means "my leg" and *miguu yangu* means "my legs" in Swahili. In Nyakyusa language, "my leg" is *kilundi kyangu* or *ikilundi kyangu*, and *ifilundi fyangu* means "my legs."

Indumbula jangu or *umojo gwangu* means "my heart" in Nyakyusa. In Kiswahili, *moyo wangu* means "my heart."

Nchi yetu means "our country" or "our land" in Swahili. The Nyakyusa say *ikisu kyitu*, meaning "our land."

Tunakwenda nyumbani kwetu in Kiswahili, or Swahili, means "we are going to our home," and *tunakwenda nyumbani* means "we are going home."

The Nyakyusa say *tusumwike kukaja kwitu*, meaning "we are going to our home"; and *tusumwike kukaja* means "we are going home."

Twende nyumbani means "let's go home" in Kiswahili or Swahili. In Kinyakyusa, or Nyakyusa, *tubuke kukaja* means "let's go home."

Kufuma kugu? It means "where do you come from?" in Kinyakyusa. In Kiswahili, it's *unatoka wapi?*

Tunsyilile umwipwa gwitu means "we have buried our uncle" in Kinyakyusa. In Kiswahili, they say, *tumemzika mjomba wetu*. Meaning the same thing.

Asubuhi means "morning" in Kiswahili. In Kinyakyusa, *lubunju* or *ulubunju* means "morning."

Mputi means "minister, pastor, or preacher" in Nyakyusa, while in Swahili, *mchungaji* means the same thing.

Tusali means "let's pray" or "we should pray" in Kiswahili. In Kinyakyusa, *twipute* means "let's pray" or "we should pray."

Mpeli gwitu means Our Creator (God) in Kinyakyusa. And *Kyala* also means "God" in Nyakyusa. In Swahili, *Mungu* means "God."

The word for "bird" or "birds" in Kiswahili is *ndege* – the same term is applied to aeroplanes. In Nyakyusa, "a bird" is called *injuni or njuni* depending on the context; the same term is also used in plural form. So *njuni* or *injuni* also means "birds" in Nyakyusa.

The term *njuni* also brings up interesting comparisons in a linguistic context.

The Nyakyusa who are indigenous to southwestern Tanzania close to the border with Malawi call birds, *njuni* or *injuni*. They have lived in what are now called Rungwe and Kyela districts in the Great Rift Valley for at least 500 years.

The Haya in northwestern Tanzania near the border with Uganda, hundreds of miles away from the Nyakyusa, also call birds, *njuni*.

The Kamba, even further away in eastern Kenya, also call birds, *njuni*.

And there are probably others who also use the term *njuni* for birds.

All their languages belong to the Bantu linguistic group.

Ndalama or *indalama* means "money" in Nyakyusa, while the Swahili terms for "money" is *fedha*. The Nyakyusa also call "money," *kyuma*.

But the exact term for money in Nyakyusa is *ndalama* or *indalama* depending on the context in which the word is used, while *kyuma* really means "metal" or "steel." But it is also used figuratively, meaning "money."

The Nyakyusa term, *kyuma*, is almost identical to the Swahili word, *chuma*, which also means "metal."

Mbulukutu or *imbulukutu* means "ear" or "ears" in Kinyakyusa, or Nyakyusa. In Swahili, *sikio* means "ear," and *masikio* means "ears."

Nkulu gwangu means "my elder brother" in Nyakyusa. In Swahili, it's *kaka yangu*.

Ndaga fiijo in Nyakyusa means "thank you very much." In Swahili, *asante sana* means "thank you very much."

So, there are some differences in Bantu languages or languages of Bantu origin.

Yet similarities abound. For example, in Kiswahili, *njia* means "way" or "path," as opposed to "road." In

Kinyakyusa, it's *njila*.

Swahili for "chicken" is *kuku*; Nyakyusa – *nguku*.

Nyama means "meat" in Swahili and Nyakyusa and in many other Bantu languages including Xhosa. The Nyakyusa also say *inyama*, meaning "meat," depending on the context in which the term is used.

Among the Nyakyusa, *imbututu* is a kind of very large black bird with red beaks which exists in real life and which I saw many times when I lived in Nyakyusaland; while among the Xhosa, *impundudu* is a mystical, huge lightning bird that is an integral part of their traditional beliefs.

And *mvua* means "rain" in Swahili, while in Nyakyusa it's called *fula*.

In Sotho, also known as Southern Sotho spoken in Lesotho and South Africa especially in the Free State Province, the word for "crocodile" is *koena*. In Nyakyusa language, "crocodile" is *ngwina*. The two terms, *koena* and *ngwina*, sound pretty close.

Those are just some examples. There are many others in many other African languages as well.

All those terms cited here, in Nyakyusa and Swahili, have their counterparts with almost the same spelling and the same meaning in many other Bantu languages which differ from Most West African languages – such as Igbo, Yoruba, Ewe, Wolof, and Twi - in many respects although they all belong to the Niger-Congo family.

Then there's the concept or philosophy of *ubuntu* as it is known in South Africa, a black African term.

Ubuntu is a belief or philosophy whose essence is the virtue of being humane. As South African writer Jordan Ngubane states in his book *An African Explains Apartheid*:

"Life in these (Sutu-nguni) had been dominated by a religious system that regarded each individual personality as sacred.

Way back in infinity, long before there was the sun or

the moon or the stars or the earth, there was Mvelinqangi, the First-to-appear, who was neither matter nor visible. He could not be seen by the naked eye because the subtle substance that constituted his body stretched from infinity to infinity.

He was eternal and creative; he was the ultimate reality from which all things were to derive their being.

He willed that there should be the sun and other planets; that there should be man, animals. Birds, stones, and trees. All were manifestations of his infinite form. Inside his being was an infinity of specialized forms making up a part of the whole. These were the spirits of living things, some of which had human forms. When they were clothed in flesh, they became the human beings who inhabited the earth....

Each human being was made up of three elements – the Mvelinqangi essence, the spirit form, and the physical body. The human always had a dual existence. When he lived, it was in the siritual and physical worlds. At death, he did not 'die'; he merely discarded the physical body and returned to his ancestors, the spirit forms....

As a future spirit form or idlozi, the individual personality had a sacredness that was absolute and immutable. He was the individualized essence of Mvelinqangi. The concept of equality in the African community was based on this evaluation of the human personality....

From such an evaluation (of man as an individualized essence of Mvelinqangi) sprang an important ethical code, which prescribed that the good life was the one in which individuality was treated with reverence and consideration. The most heinous crime in the Zulu state, for example, was witchcraft, not murder. Zulu law took the attitude that in murder the criminal merely separated body and soul; in witchcraft, the miscreant interfered with the most sacred ingredient in the human makeup.

Supreme virtue lay in being humane, in accepting the

human being as a part of yourself, with a right to be denied nothing that you possessed. It was inhuman to drive the hungry stranger from your door, for your neighbor's sorrow was yours.

This code constituted a philosophy of life, and the great Sutu-nguni family – Bantu has political connotations that the Africans resent – called it, significantly, *ubuntu* or *botho* (pronounced *butu*), the practice of being humane.

The harshest judgment that the humblest African in the Sutu-nguni community can make of his neighbor is to say that he is not humane. The nearest equivalent to this value judgment in the West is to say a person is not civilized or morally developed.

This philosophy gave content to life in the Sutu-nguni states before the advent of the white man.

Defeat (by the white man) shattered the political and social institutions that gave visible expression to this attitude. Disaster could not, however, penetrate so deeply into the African's being as to destroy those things he prized most – the perspectives from which he viewed life and which gave it meaning.

These remained deep in his self, giving him spiritual sustenance in moments of trial. He has always clung to them with a determination that nothing seems capable of cracking." - (Jordan Ngubane, *An African Explains Apartheid*, quoted by Godfrey Mwakikagile, *Africa and The West*, Huntington, New York: Nova Science Publishers, Inc., 2000, pp. 20 21; 21 – 22, from Jordan Ngubane, *An African Explains Apartheid*, New York: Pall Mall, 1963, pp. 75 – 76; 76 – 77).

The Nyakyusa and other Africans have the same belief, what black South Africans call *ubuntu*, but use different terms to define it. Yet there are striking similarities in the terms used among many of them.

While black South Africans say *ubuntu*, the Nyakyusa say *ubundu*, sometimes simply *bundu* depending on the context; hardly any difference even in linguistic terms between what black South Africans call *ubuntu* and what the Nyakyusa of Tanzania and Malawi call *ubundu* or *bundu*.

In Kiswahili, or Swahili, it is called *utu*.

All those linguistic and philosophical similarities clearly point to a common origin of these people and their languages as members of the Niger-Congo family who migrated from what is today eastern Nigeria and Cameroon about 2000 years ago and spread throughout East, Central and Southern Africa.

There are still more similarities. For example, according to studies done by British anthropologists Godfrey Wilson and Monica Wilson, who were husband and wife, the Venda of South Africa and the Nyakyusa of Tanzania and Malawi also have many strong cultural similarities.

Godfrey Wilson's study, "The Nyakyusa of South-Western Tanganyika," is contained in a book, *Seven Tribes of Central Africa*, published in 1951.

And some of the best anthropological studies ever conducted in the field were done by Monica Wilson on the Nyakyusa and published as books, *Good Company: A Study of Nyakyusa Age-Villages*, and *Rituals of Kinship Among the Nyakyusa*, among other works by her on the Nyakyusa and other tribes in the region.

The Venda are also related to the Lemba of South Africa and Zimbabwe who, according to genetic (DNA) evidence, are also partly Jewish, tracing part of their heritage to Yemen more than 2,000 years ago.

But in spite of being partly Jewish, the Lemba are predominantly of Bantu stock, and their language is related to other Bantu languages in East, Central and Southern Africa.

The Lemba became part of the Venda community long after the Venda had settled in the region. They believe that they are Black Jews and descendants of the lost tribe of

Israel. They usually keep to themselves and only marry within their own group.

They also sometimes refer to themselves as *Vhalungu*, which means "non-Negroid" or "respected foreigner." But this is just a form of inferiority complex on their part, ashamed of what they are as a black African people. Although they have some Jewish genes, they are mostly black African of "Negro" stock or origin some of them despise so much.

And there area lot of things all these communities have in common as an African people.

In fact many of these ethnic groups – or tribes – use identical terms in many cases to identify the same objects and natural phenomena.

It is from such linguistic similarities that the term Bantu is derived to identify the people who speak these related languages. And the term Bantu – or any other term similar to that – simply means "people"; except that in this case the term Bantu means "these particular people"and not just any other people.

The term Bantu – as a collective term used to identify the people mostly in East, Central and Southern Africa who speak related languages – was coined in the 1850s by W.H.I. Bleek, a librarian of the British government of the Cape Colony and has been used since then, although it had derogatory connotations during the apartheid era.

And because of its racist connotations in the past, most blacks in South Africa don't accept the term when it's used to identify them as a people or as individuals who are members of the Bantu family of ethnic groups. In fact, in the minds of most black South Africans, it's still a pejorative term even today.

But it is widely used in other parts of Africa - East and Central - without any problems to identify Bantu speakers. However, it must be emphasised that there is no Bantu race. "Bantu" is, simply, a linguistic term more than anything else.

The Bantu linguistic group has more than 200 languages belonging to the Niger-Congo family. They include Kiswahili (Swahili), Zulu and Xhosa; the latter two being the most prominent black African languages spoken in South Africa by the country's two largest black ethnic groups.

The Bantu were agriculturalists and they developed their own complex community organisations which came into collision with European cultures when Europeans settled in South Africa and other parts of the continent. And South Africa became the scene of some of the bloodiest conflicts between Africans and Europeans.

After Bartolomeau Dias became the first European to round the Cape of Good Hope (originally named the Cape of Storms), other navigators and explorers followed, including Vasco da Gama. What they found, saw and recorded was highly significant in terms of history and clash of civilisations between Africa and the West.

There were some people who years later claimed there were no Africans when the first European settlers arrived in South Africa. The presence of the San and the Khoikhoi proved them wrong. So did the presence of the Bantu who preceded whites in other parts of South Africa.

The diaries of shipwrecked Portuguese sailors attest to a large Bantu-speaking population in present-day KwaZulu-Natal by 1552. There is no question that Africans had settled there long before Europeans arrived in that part of South Africa, despite claims to the contrary by those who want to re-write history.

The Portuguese frequently passed by South Africa on their way to East Africa – mainly to what is Mozambique today, and sometimes to what became Tanzania and Kenya – and India. They even stopped for some rest and to pick up some food and other provisions for the long sea journeys. But no permanent European settlement was established anywhere in South Africa until 1652 when Jan van Riebeeck and about 90 other persons set up a provisioning station for the Dutch East India Company at Table Bay on the Cape of Good Hope.

It was a milestone in the history of South Africa and the beginning of a new era of European colonisation of this part of the African continent.

Soon thereafter, Jan van Riebeeck began to trade with the indigenous people in the area, the Khoikhoi. He also acquired large areas of fertile land and gave it to European settlers for farms. He also brought in Africans from West and East Africa as well as Malays from Malaysia and used them as slaves working for white settlers. The indigenous people, the Khoikhoi and the San, were also enslaved.

By 1662, there were about 250 Europeans living near the Cape. They gradually moved inland and founded Stellenbosch in 1679.

In 1689, about 200 Huguenot refugees arrived from Europe. They were mostly French Huguenots and they went on to establish a thriving wine industry in the region. They also intermarried with the Dutch settlers who had arrived earlier.

By 1707 there were about 1,780 freeholders of European descent in South Africa, and they owned about 1,100 slaves, mostly African.

The foundation for the establishment of a white-dominated society had been laid, and it had a devastating impact on African communities for the next 300 years.

By the early part of the 1700s, most of the San had migrated to other parts of the country. They fled from European domination and chose inaccessible regions for sanctuary to make sure that Europeans would not follow them. The other group of Africans indigenous to that part of South Africa also adopted survival techniques. They far outnumbered the San. Some of them chose to remain near the Cape, while others dispersed into the interior.

As the different groups were adjusting or re-adjusting themselves, with some of them staking out new claims of territory, tragedy struck. A great smallpox outbreak in

1713 killed many European settlers and most of the Khoikhoi who lived near the Cape.

During the same period, a new society was evolving around the Cape, involving racial intermarriage.

In the 1700s, intermarriage between Khoikhoi slaves and European settlers began to create what came to be known as the Coloured population. At the same time, white farmers – known as Boers or Afrikaners – began to trek (journey) increasingly farther from the Cape in search of pasture and farmland.

It was another important milestone in the history of South Africa and came to be known as the Boer trek. It had profound impact on the evolution of the South African society or of South Africa as a country and as a nation and played a critical role in determining the nature of race relations for generations.

By 1750, some white farmers had migrated to the region between the Gamtoos and Great Fish rivers, where they encountered the Xhosa, the second-largest ethnic group after the Zulu to whom they are also closely related. It was another turning point in South African history.

At first the encounters were friendly. Whites and blacks engaged in commerce, exchanging goods, and sometimes goods from Europeans for labour from Africans. But in 1789, the first of a long series of Xhosa Wars broke out between them. The conflicts were mostly over land and catle ownership. White settlers wanted to establish the Great Fish River as the southern frontier of the Xhosa nation. The Xhosa refused to accept that. They knew their land more than Europeans did. And the stage was set for another conflict.

That was the beginning of almost 100 years of war between Europeans and the Xhosa in one of the longest campaigns of resistance against European domination by Africans. The wars were fought in 1789, 1799, 1812, 1819, 1834, 1846, 1850, and 1877.

The late Jordan Ngubane, a South African journalist

and author, in his book *An African Explains Apartheid*, is one of the people who have written eloquently about African resistance to white domination in South Africa. And he wrote with pride about the Xhosa and the way they resisted white domination during the 100 years of war in their native land and the land of their ancestors. It was a campaign, among several others, whose memory Africans invoked through the years during their struggle against apartheid.

While white settlers were waging military campaigns against Africans, they also had their own conflicts within. It was a house divided. The conflict was between the British and the Boers.

During the French Revolutionary and Napoleonic wars, the British replaced the Dutch at the Cape as the dominant force from 1795 to 1803, and again from 1806 to 1814, when the territory was assigned to Great Britain by the Congress of Vienna.

In 1820, 5,000 British settlers were given small farms near the Great Fish River. The farms were intended to form a buffer zone and a barrier to the southern movement of the Xhosa, but most of the British settlers soon gave up farming and moved to nearby towns such as Port Elizabeth and Grahamstown. Their arrival and settlement in South Africa was another important milestone in the history of the country.

They were the first large group of European settlers not to be assimilated into the Afrikaner culture that evolved in the 17th and 18th centuries and they changed the demographic configuration of the white settler community. It was, before then, a homogeneous or monolithic whole. But with their arrival, it now became two communities of whites in what was gradually becoming a new nation dominated by whites, although predominantly black.

There was also a conflict of perceptions and realities between the two groups. The Afrikaner or Boer community – or one dominated by them – was very conservative and opposed to any kind of improvement in the lives of Africans and Coloureds, although even back then Coloureds were given preferential treatment over blacks who were considered to be the most inferior.

The British, on the other hand, were not opposed to that, although they also, like the Boers, did not believe that blacks and Coloureds were entitled to racial equality across the spectrum.

But they alienated the Boers by restructuring the administration of the Cape Colony along British lines, by calling for better treatment of the Coloureds and blacks who worked for the Boers as servants or slaves, by granting free nonwhites legal rights equal to those of the whites, and by restricting the acquisition of new land by Boers who robbed blacks of their right to land ownership they had always enjoyed before Europeans came.

And in 1833, the British further infuriated the Boers when they abolished slavery throughout the British Empire, including the Cape Colony.

A disproportionately large number of slave owners were Boers – or Afrikaners – but other whites also owned a significant number of slaves who were mostly African. Although the emancipation of slaves angered South African slave owners, they were consoled by the fact that the freed slaves remained oppressed and continued to be exploited by white land owners.

The transfer of power from the Dutch to the British in the Cape Colony, and the restrictions the British rulers imposed on the Dutch community, led to another development which became critical to the future of the country.

To escape British domination and the restrictions imposed on them by the British rulers, about 12,000 Boers left the Cape Colony between 1835 and 1843 in what came to be known as the Great Trek.

The Voortrekkers, as the Boer trekkers are called in Afrikaans (the language of Afrikaners), migrated beyond the Orange River. Some remained in the highveld of the interior, forming isolated communities and small states highly defensive of the Afrikaner way of life. And a large group travelled eastwards into what became Natal.

In February 1838, 70 Boers were killed in Natal by Zulu forces led by Dingane. In December the same year, Andries Pretorius (after whom the capital Pretoria was named) defeated the Zulu in one of the bloodiest conflicts in South African history, the Battle of the Blood River, during which the water of the river turned red with blood from the Zulus killed during the conflict. And the Boers proceeded to establish farms in Natal.

But fortunes changed again. Britain annexed Natal in 1843, depriving the Boers one of their most prized possessions. After the annexation, most of the Boers left Natal and returned to the interior. Natal gradually became a British stronghold and the most British province in South Africa.

The Boers were undeterred, in spite of the defeat and humiliation they had suffered at the hands of the British, and in the 1850s went on to establish the Boer republics of the Orange Free State and the Transvaal. This was nother critical development in the history of South Africa.

Yet another important milestone was the arrival of the first indentured labourers in the country. They came from India and arrived in Natal in 1860 to work on the sugar plantations. The coming of the Indians would later have a dramatic impact on the country and forever change the face of South Africa.

The Indians changed the demographic composition of the country and became the largest non-black ethnic group in Natal. By 1900, they outnumbered whites in that province. Even today, Natal has the largest Indian population in South Africa.

The history of South Africa in the early years was also shaped by its abundant resources. Some of the resources which played a critical role in the transformation of the country were minerals. And they still determine the fate of South Africa today.

In 1867, diamonds were discovered along the Vaal and Orange rivers. More were discovered in 1871 at what became Kimberley. And in 1886, gold was discovered on the Witwatersrand.

All these discoveries, especially the discovery of gold, spurred great economic development in South Africa between 1870 and 1900. Foreign trade increased dramatically, more roads, railways and other infrastructure were built, and the number of whites sharply rose from 300,000 in 1870 to about 1 million in 1900.

While all this was going on, dramatic changes were also taking place in the political arena. In 1871 the British annexed the rich diamond-mining region of Griqualand West despite protests by the Boers in Orange Free State of which this region was an integral part. Then in 1877, they also annexed Transvaal. But the Boers revolted and Transvaal regained its independence in 1881.

In 1889, another important political development took place. The British-ruled Cape Colony and the Boer-dominated Orange Free State formed a customs union but Transvaal, led by Paul Kruger, adamantly refused to be a part of it.

Then there emerged on the scene a political figure who would have an impact beyond the borders of South Africa for many years. That was Cecil Rhodes.

His name still conjures up images from the past, and his presence is still felt in many ways even today, including the land crisis in Zimbabwe, a country that probably would not have existed as it does today, or become what it did, had it not been for him and his adventures and imperial ambitions which took him into regions far beyond the Cape and outside South Africa.

Besides his ambition to expand the British empire, Cecil Rhodes was also a staunch advocate of federation in South Africa. In 1890, he became prime minister of the

Cape Colony, a position which enabled him to pursue his goals and implement policies which also had a profound impact on the future of South Africa.

He was determined to reshape South Africa and, by 1894, he was busy encouraging non-Afrikaner whites – known as the Uitlanders – in the Transvaal to overthrow Prime Minister Paul Kruger.

In December 1895, Leander Starr Jameson, a close associate of Cecil Rhodes, invaded the Transvaal with a small force. His intention, which was also Rhodes', was to help the non-Afrikaner whites in the Transvaal in an uprising against the Boer government of Prime Minister Paul Kruger. But the uprising never took place, and Jameson's small force was defeated by early January 1896 in only a few weeks.

Tensions increased between the British and the Boers in the following years when the British government under Prime Minister Joseph Chamberlain and the British high commissioner (ambassador) in South Africa, Alfred Milner, supported the non-white Afrikaners (the Uitlanders) against the dominant Afrikaners. It was clear the two sides were headed for war.

In 1896, the Boer colonies of the Transvaal and the Orange Free State formed an alliance. And in 1899, they declared war on Britain.

It was the beginning of one of the bloodiest conflicts in African colonial history. The conflict was called the South African War but also came to be known as the Boer War. It was fought from 1899 to 1902 and was won by the British.

It was also the British who were involved in another major conflict, Mau Mau, years later which was compared to the Boer War. As George Padmore stated in his book, *Pan-African or Communism? The Coming Struggle for Africa*, published in 1956 when Mau Mau was going on:

> What started as an 'emergency' has already become a full-scale military operation – the biggest colonial war in Africa since the Boer

War. - (George Padmore, *Pan-Africanism or Communism?* (London: Dennis Dobson), p. 254).

Not only was it a major conflict; it changed the course of South African history. The Afrikaners never forgot their loss and humiliation and it helped fuel Afrikaner nationalism which culminated in the establishment of apartheid years later, making white-dominated South Africa one of the most racist countries in the history of mankind.

With the British now firmly in control, the transformation of South Africa began in earnest. In 1910, the Union of South Africa was established. It included the Cape of Good Hope, Natal, the Orange Free State, and the Transvaal as provinces.

It was a unitary state as stipulated by the constitution. Also under the union constitution, the Dutch language – and later in 1925 Afrikaans as well – had equal status with English, and each province retained its existing franchise qualifications. The Cape already allowed some nonwhites to votes but the other provinces did not.

The establishment of the Union of South Africa also underscored one very important point.

White people, in spite of the conflicts they had – especially between the British and the Boers – submerged their differences to secure their interests and created a white-dominated society in which Africans had no rights equal to whites. This bond among whites was also an important lesson for blacks. It clearly showed that without unity among blacks, there was no hope for fundamental change in South Africa and the country would continue to be dominated by whites.

Only two years later, in 1912, African leaders from all over the country, and from all walks of life, met in Bloemfontein to form an organisation which would fight for their rights as one people regardless of their tribal or ethnic differences. That was the beginning of the African

National Congress (ANC) which 80 years later finally ended white domination.

Nelson Mandela, in his book *Long walk to Freedom*, paid tribute to the founders of the African National Congress who met in Bloemfontein in 1912, and to all those who went before him, for the sacrifices they made in the struggle for freedom and racial equality which almost 100 years later enabled him and others to finally walk and live free in the land of their homeland.

The Union of South Africa also led to the evolution of the most advanced country on the African continent.

After elections were held in 1910, Louis Botha, an Afrikaner, became the first prime minister of the Union of South Africa. He led the South African party which was an amalgam of Afrikaner parties which advocated close cooperation between Afrikaners and South Africans of British descent. And in 1912, J.B.M. Hertzog founded the Afrikaner-oriented National Party. It was this party which almost 50 years later instituted apartheid.

Even before the diabolical institution of apartheid, racial discrimination was a way of life in South Africa, with Africans suffering the most. But it did not have the legal underpinnings across the spectrum apartheid had years later.

Efforts were made to fight discrimination and one of the most important figures in this struggle on the South African scene was Mahatma Gandhi. He led a relentless campaign against racial injustices and, as a leader in the Indian community, he played a major role in helping alleviate the plight of the Indians in South Africa. By 1914, the Indians were receiving somewhat better treatment than before, and were even accorded rights black people never had and which they only dreamed of.

The year 1914 was also critical in the history of the world. It was the year in which the First World War started and Prime Minister Louis Botha led South Africa into the war on the side of the Allies. He also quickly suppressed a revolt by Afrikaners who were opposed to his policy of supporting the Allies.

The following year witnessed the expansion of South Africa as the dominant force in the region and as a true supporter of the Allied forces against Germany. In 1915, South African forces captured South West Africa, what is Namibia today, from the Germans. South West Africa was then a German colony.

After the war, the territory was placed under the Union of South Africa as a League of Nations mandate.

It remained under South African control for more than 70 years even after the League of Nations was replaced by the United Nations (UN) The apartheid regime refused to relinquish control of the territory in spite of the resolutions passed by the UN terminating its mandate over the former German colony.

In 1919, Louis Botha was succeeded as prime minister by J.C. Smuts, his close associate. It was also a period of unrest at the mines and consolidation of white rule over blacks and other non-whites. Between 1921 and 1922, skilled mine workers on the Witwatersrand organised a major strike to protect their jobs. They were worried about losing their jobs to lower-paid nonwhites. Prime Minister Smuts was determined to end the strike and he used troops to suppress the strikers, but at a heavy price. At least 230 people were killed.

The violence had great implications for the future of South Africa, leading to the election of J.B.M. Hertzog as prime minister in 1924. He remained in office until 1939, which was also the beginning of World War II.

But the two leaders – Smuts and Hertzog – were not enemies, although Hertzog replaced Smuts as prime minister. From 1934 to 1939, Smuts supported Hertzog and the two leaders went on to form the United South African National Party.

Prime Minister Hertzog played a major in shaping the destiny of the Afrikaner community in South Africa. More than anybody else before him, he led an Afrikaner cultural and economic revival which improved the overall well-being of Afrikaners who felt that they had been pushed to the periphery by the British.

He was also influential in gaining additional British recognition of South African independence – through the Balfour Declaration of 1926 and the Statute of Westminster of 1931. South Africa became a legal sovereign entity in 1934.

And in December 1932, he took South Africa off the gold standard, thus raising the price of gold and stimulating the gold-mining industry and the economy in general.

But Prime Minister Hertzog will also always be remembered for paving the way for apartheid because of the policies he implemented. He was, in fact, one of the architects of apartheid.

He curtailed and restricted the rights of nonwhites in many areas of life including the right to vote; he expanded the creation of reserves for blacks as their permanent homes, and he regulated their movement in the remainder of the country where they were not even considered to be citizens but mere guests and expendable commodity good only for serving whites by providing them with cheap labour.

But the alliance between Hertzog and Smuts did not last much longer. It fell apart because of their differences over World War War II. They differed on whether or not to support Britain in the war.

In September 1939, Smuts won a crucial vote in parliament and was back in office as prime minister. He was already on the British side and with his renewed mandate as prime minister, he brought South Africa into the war supporting Britain and the Allied forces.

Hertzog, on the other hand, was resolutely opposed to South African involvement in the war in support of the Allies. He had little affection for Great Britain and was not worried about the Nazis; which was interpreted as sympathy for Nazi Germany. In fact, South Africa already had many Nazi sympathisers, especially among the Afrikaners. And Hertzog himself was an Afrikaner and one of the staunchest supporters of Afrikaner causes.

But nothing could be done to stop South Africa from going to war, and South African troops played a very important role in the conflict. They fought with distinction in Italy and Madagascar, and helped to end Italian control of Ethiopia which was invaded by Musollini in 1936.

South African involvement in the war, which was opposed by many Afrikaners, helped to galvanise the Afrikaner community. It was yet another reminder of how powerless they were at the hands of the British in South Africa. They also resented the more liberal policy towards nonwhites pursued by some South Africans of British descent and even by a few Afrikaners such as Jan Hofmeyr.

Hofmeyr was a close associate of Smuts and he supported policies which would give nonwhites more rights although not equal to whites. But even that was bad enough in the eyes of most Afrikaners and other whites. And that set the stage for the 1948 general election whose results would change South Africa as never before.

The Afrikaner-dominated National Party won the election, and D.F. Malan became prime minister. He served from 1948 to 1954. It was during his tenure that the government instituted apartheid as official policy.

In fact, apartheid also became a religion. Whites were taught and many of them believed that blacks were inferior to them. Even some ministers of the Dutch Reformed Church preached from the pulpit the separation of the races and about the inferiority of black people as no more than hewers of wood and drawers of water for whites who had been "ordained" by God - had the *divine* mandate - to rule members of "the lesser breed", especially black people.

Apartheid became the lasting legacy of the National Party, and the party remained in power until the early 1990s when apartheid was formally ended.

Dr. Malan was succeeded by J.G. Strijdom who served as prime minister from 1954 to 1958. He was succeeded by Hendrick Verwoerd whose tenure lasted from 1958 to 1966 when he was assassinated – stabbed to death – by a discontented white employee whom the authorities later described as deranged man.

Verwoerd was succeeded by John Vorster who served from 1966 to 1978. And "The Great Crocodile," P.W. Botha, the last of the "great" architects and enforcers of apartheid, served as prime minister from 1978 to 1989. He was one of the most ruthless leaders apartheid ever produced.

Botha was also responsible for launching military attacks on neighbouring countries which supported the freedom fighters, whom the apartheid regime called "terrorists." The military strikes targeted the offices and training camps of the freedom fighters but also entailed heavy collateral damage. The apartheid regime also deliberately targeted installations and other infrastructure of the neighbouring countries to stop or discourage them from harbouring the freedom fighters.

All that was in pursuit of the apartheid regime's policy of "hot pursuit," going after the freedom fighters. And Botha was good at it. In fact, as far back as August 1968, when he was defence minister, he issued an ominous warning to countries which he said harboured "terrorists." He said "they should receive a sudden hard knock" – quoted by Colin Legum and John Drysdale in *Africa Contemporary Record 1968 – 1969* – in pointed reference to Tanzania and Zambia.

He pursued the policies of his predecessors with diligence and religious zeal and went even further, much further, in clamping down on the opponents of apartheid.

It was these leaders who played the biggest role in

consolidating white domination and in enforcing apartheid in all areas of national life. And they remained unrepentant until their last days. As Botha bluntly stated after apartheid ended, he and other whites who supported and enforced apartheid had nothing to apologise for.

But, in spite of the iron-fisted rule black people and other nonwhites had to endure under apartheid, the victims of this racial injustice did not give up fighting for their rights and were, in fact, inspired even more to take an uncompromising stand against racial oppression and exploitation in their quest for justice, no matter what the cost. And many of them, including school children as happened in Soweto in June 1976, lost their lives.

Organised protest against racial injustice started back in 1912 when the African National Congress was formed. The Industrial and Commercial Workers Union of South Africa founded in 1919 by Clement Kadalie who originally came from Nyasaland (renamed Malawi at independence in 1966) also played a very important role in fighting racial injustice.

After apartheid was formally instituted in 1948, protests continued in the 1950s. They also went on in the sixties but mainly in the early part of the decade before the government banned the African National Congress and the Pan-Africanist Congress which was formed in 1959 as an offshoot of the ANC.

The protests involved passive resistance through peaceful demonstrations. They also involved burning passbooks.

In 1960, a peaceful protest against the pass laws organised by the Pan-Africanist Congress – an organisation led by Mangaliso Robert Sobukwe - at Sharpeville ended in violence when the police opened fire on the unarmed protesters, killing 69. The apartheid regime drew international condemnation for the killings and the incident came to be immortalised as the Sharpeville Massacre.

It was one of the most important events in the struggle against apartheid and galvanised the opponents of the regime into action in a way they had never been before. It was a turning point in the history of South Africa and the opponents who had earlier used non-violent tactics to pursue their goals now embraced violence as the last resort.

After the African National Congress (ANC), the Pan-Africanist Congress (PAC) and the South African Communist Party (SACP) were banned, they went underground to continue the struggle which now included guerrilla warfare against the regime.

The South African Communist Party was mostly white and it found allies among many blacks because it accepted them as equals. White communists were among the few whites in South Africa who openly campaigned for racial equality and supported blacks and other non-whites in their struggle against racial injustices. The SACP was equally committed to the destruction of apartheid and worked in alliance with the ANC to destroy this racist edifice; a diabolical institution which had its biggest support among Afrikaners.

The two remained allies throughout the struggle and, after apartheid was abolished, the South African Communist Party became a partner in the ANC-led government. They remain allies even today.

But all these organisations and other anti-apartheid groups were virtually decapitated in the early sixties when most of their leaders were either in prison, in exile, or neutralised within, as the government also proceeded with its plans to segregate blacks on a more permanent basis by restricting them to designated areas. Their movement was also severely curtailed.

While all this was going on, the regime also faced problems internationally because of its racist policies and brutal mistreatment of blacks and other nonwhites.

In 1961, South Africa left the Commonwealth – an

association composed of Britain and her former colonies – because of severe criticism of her racist policies by many countries.

One of the strongest opponents of the apartheid regime was Julius Nyerere. In August 1960, which was many months before he led Tanganyika to independence from Britain in December 1961, he made it clear that Tanganyika would not join the Commonwealth after gaining independence if South Africa remained a member of the Commonwealth. As he put it: "To vote South Africa in, is to vote us out."

He is credited with having playing a major role in forcing South Africa out of the Commonwealth and went on to become the most prominent African leader in independent Africa – besides Dr. Kwame Nkrumah who was overthrown in February in 1966 in a coup masterminded by the CIA – in support of the liberation movements in the white-ruled countries of Southern Africa.

In May 1963, the Organisation of African Unity (OAU) chose Dar es Salaam, Tanzania's capital, to be the headquarters of all the African liberation movements under the leadership of Nyerere. And he lived long enough to see South Africa, the bastion of white supremacy on the continent, finally free and attended the inauguration of Nelson Mandela as the country's first democratically elected president. He died of leukemia in October 1999 at the age of 77.

After South Africa was forced to leave the Commonwealth, it became a republic. It became the Republic of South Africa on 31 May 1961 and left the Commonwealth six months later.

The apartheid regime also became embroiled in a dispute with the United Nations and many countries in the sixties and thereafter because of its refusal to relinquish control of South West Africa.

The apartheid regime believed it had the right to

control, rule and exploit South West Africa. In fact, after the end of World War II and the demise of the League of Nations, South Africa presented to the United Nations in 1946 a plan to annex South West Africa. That was only about two years before the National Party, the achitect of apartheid, came to power in 1948.

The UN rejected the proposal, insisting that South Africa submit to a UN trusteeship for the contested territory.

On 27 October 1966, the UN General Assembly adopted a resolution stating that South Africa had forfeited its mandatory rights to South West Africa. And two years later, the General Assembly resolved that South West Africa would henceforth be known as Namibia. But the apartheid regime refused to accept either resolution.

In 1971, the World Court handed down an advisory opinion that South Africa had no jurisdiction over South West Africa and should withdraw its administration. It did not.

Black nationalists formed the South West African People's Organisation (SWAPO) to fight for independence and the UN recognised SWAPO as the authoritative representative of the Namibian people.

On 31 January 1976, the UN Security Council unanimously approved a resolution calling for UN-supervised elections in Namibia. And the General Assembly approved a resolution in December 1976 endorsing "armed struggle" by blacks to win independence from the apartheid regime which also ruled their country.

On 17 June, 1985, South Africa restored internal self-rule to Namibia bu forbade Namibia's legislature from passing "any laws altering the international status of the territory."

Thus, South Africa remained in full control of Namibia even after 1985.

But, in spite of the regime's intransigence over South West Africa through the years, the South African government did, under the leadership of Prime Minister John Vorster, attempt in the sixties and seventies to forge links with other independent African countries in order to conduct dialogue on racial problems in South Africa and on other matters of mutual concern.

However, Vorster's diplomatic initiatives achieved very little besides the establishment of diplomatic relations with Malawi and close economic - and to a smaller extent political - ties with Lesotho, Botswana and Swaziland all of which were economically dependent on South Africa and found it impossible to sever those ties. In fact, those ties already existed, for historical reasons, and Vorster only tried to strengthen them.

In the seventies, the struggle for independence in some of the neighbouring countries gained momentum and the apartheid regime was strongly opposed to the establishment of black rule in those countries. The countries were Rhodesia, a British colony; Mozambique, and Angola both of which were Portuguese colonies. Lesotho, Botswana and Swaziland were already independent, having gained independence in the late sixties, and they all were former British colonies.

South Africa tried to stem the tide, and derail the independence movement in Rhodesia, Mozambique and Angola by providing military assistance to the colonial governments in those countries which were at war with the freedom fighters. But nothing could stop the struggle for freedom.

By late 1974, it was clear that Mozambique and Angola would be independent in a few months and South Africa, as one of the few remaining white-ruled nations of Africa, faced the grim prospect of being further isolated from the international community.

The apartheid regime was also further isolated in regional context, of Southern Africa, when both Mozambique and Angola won independence in 1975 after more than 500 years of Portuguese colonial rule. The only true ally the regime had in Africa was neighbouring Rhodesia which was still under white-minority rule. But even this one was coming under increasing pressure from the freedom fighters, other African countries and the international community to end white domination, although it was not until April 1980 that Rhodesia finally became free as the new nation of Zimbabwe.

Even within South Africa itself, opposition to the apartheid regime increased in the seventies. Some of the most visible opponents of white-minority rule were white students who in the early 1970s became more actively involved, and in larger numbers, in the struggle against apartheid together with other whites opposed to the regime's racist policies.

The National Party itself, which instituted apartheid, was divided over the party's policies on race relations. There was the somewhat liberal wing – known as *verligte*, which in Afrikaans means "enlightened" - pitted against the conservative group known as *verkrampte* which means "narrow-minded."

The differences between the two did not split the party, since both were basically in agreement on continuation of white rule But it was clear that the ruling party faced prospects of further alienation from an important segment of the white community if the regime did not change or soften some of its racial policies towards nonwhites and give them some freedom, and restrain the apartheid forces from brutalising blacks and other opponents of apartheid. The liberal wing of the party felt that the government only made matters worse by being so harsh towards nonwhites and others who were against its policies.

This was in a country where the police could arrest and imprison people without a court order and hold them indefinitely without letting them communicate with lawyers, family members or friends. Or they could be "banned" to their homes and denied rights of free speech and visits by other family members and friends. And the security police were protected from court restrains and could not even be prosecuted in most cases, if at all.

This was also in a country where less than 1 person in 5 was white. Yet whites controlled the government and all aspects of life under apartheid. To enforce apartheid, parliament passed restrictive racial laws in the 1950s and 1960s and it was these laws which radicalised many of the opponents of apartheid turning them into militants.

South Africa under apartheid was a country in which about two-thirds of the blacks lived on tribal reserves which covered only about 13 per cent of the country's land. And much of that was barren, while whites owned the rest and most of the fertile areas.

Millions of blacks were forcibly moved from "white" areas to nine homelands: Bophuthatswana, Ciskei, Gazankulu, KwaZulu, Lebowa, Qwaqwa, Swazi, Transkei, and Venda. Life was hard in these homelands. There was no employment or enough facilities, including schools and hospitals, for black people many of whom had been removed from the so-called white areas where they had better life.

In the early seventies, black workers staged strikes and violently revolted against their inferior conditions. This was mostly in the cities where those who had jobs were allowed to live but under the highly restrictive pass laws. Still, the apartheid regime refused to compromise let alone change its policies.

It also refused to abandon its policy on homelands for blacks. In 1976, the apartheid regime granted sovereign status to Transkei; to Bophutatswana in 1977, to Venda in 1979, and to Ciskei in 1981. But no country recognised them as sovereign entities. Only the apartheid regime did. Other countries including the United Nations contended that all of South Africa was one country. They also saw the homelands programme as part of the government's apartheid policy intended to segregate the races even further.

The policy on homelands required blacks who were members of tribes which had "independent" homelands to give up their South African citizenship, even though they were born and brought up, and lived in South Africa. The intention was that by the time all the homelands were "independent," most blacks would no longer be citizens of South Africa. And whites would then be the majority of South African citizens. The entire South Africa then had about 5 million whites out of a total population of about 27 million, mostly black.

The homelands were nothing but tribal reserves similar to Indian reservations in the United States for Native Americans. Wholly dependent on white-ruled South Africa for their economic existence, the homelands were "landlocked islands" surrounded by lands and communities controlled by whites.

Even migrant blacks who were allowed to live and work in the cities were deprived of many basic human rights. They were forbidden to bring their wives and children with them. They were also, together with permanent black families resident in the cities, forced to live in "locations" - shanty towns such as Soweto, Alexandra, and Crossroads - set aside on the outskirts of cities and or towns. The cities and towns were mostly for whites, a constant reminder of the brutal segregation of the races under apartheid.

Asians and those of mixed ancestry called Coloureds were similarly restricted to specific living areas. But they were treated better than blacks in many areas of national life. Schools were also segregated, except a few private ones.

Most professional and supervisory jobs were held by whites, while blacks were restricted to jobs requiring unskilled and semiskilled labour on farms, in mines, in manufacturing plants, and in public service, regardless of their educational qualifications. And they were grossly underpaid.

Despite protests against apartheid and international condemnation of South Africa's diabolical policies, the regime continued its rigid policy of racial segregation. And in November 1974, the UN General Assembly suspended South Africa's voting privileges in the international organisation as a way of punishing the racist regime.

But the punishment was not enough. It was really more of a protest than a punishment, and the apartheid government was not in the least perturbed by that, clearly demonstrated by its defiance of international opinion against its policies, and its continued suppression of the apartheid opponents at home.

Its opponents were also in no mood to compromise, let alone give up the fight. On June 16, 1976, a wave of protest riots and strikes by students in the black township of Soweto rocked the nation. The students were protesting against the government's decision to force them to learn and use Afrikaans as the medium of instruction. They were also protesting against inferior education and lack of educational facilities and material including books.

The government responded with a vengeance. And the result was bloodshed. More than 600 students were killed and nearly 4,000 injured by the police and security forces who also used armoured vehicles to patrol Soweto and suppress the uprising. Over the next several months, rioting spread to other large cities of South Africa.

The carnage and brutal treatment of the students also sent shock waves throughout the international community and the UN General Assembly, on 4 November 1977, unanimously ordered a worldwide mandatory embargo on the shipment of military supplies to South Africa. It was the first such action ever taken by the UN against a member nation.

And in December the same year, the General Assembly adopted by huge majorities resolutions calling on the UN Security Council to impose an oil embargo on South Africa – stop all oil shipments – and to cut off foreign investment in that country.

The Soweto uprising was a critical turning point in the history of South Africa. It was probably the most critical in the long road to freedom.

Probably more than any other event before then, it marked the beginning of the end of apartheid although it still was many more years - almost 20 - before the edifice of apartheid finally came tumbling down. Still, it was the beginning of the end, and the student uprising galvanised the anti-apartheid struggle in an unprecedented way, nationally and internationally.

Only a few years after the Soweto uprising, South Africa was again hit by violence. That was in 1980. It experienced the worst wave of racial violence since 1976. In June 1980, guerrilla freedom fighters bombed two of the country's new coal-to-oil conversion plants and an oil refinery. Later in the same month, police fired on black demonstrators in Cape Town.

The bombing of the oil facilities was a major blow to the apartheid regime. It put a lot of investment in the project and hoped that the facilities would be the answer to South Africa's oil problems. The construction of the oil facilities was prompted by soaring oil prices, the uncertainties of depending on foreign sources for oil, and continued isolation of South Africa from the international community because of its policy of apartheid.

As the price of oil soared in 1979, the government rushed construction of several plants to convert coal into oil. The plants were expected to provide from one-third to one-half of the country's oil needs by the late 1980s.

But destruction of the oil facilities by the freedom fighters did not discourage or stop the apartheid regime from pursuing its racist policies. It also continued its policy of "hot pursuit," chasing "terrorists" - freedom fighters - all the way to where they came from in neighbouring countries where they were trained.

In 1975, South Africa invaded Angola. But the invasion

was a complete failure. South African troops also invaded Lesotho in 1982 and 1985 to kill guerrillas. Among the victims were innocent civilians including women and children. They also invaded Botswana on 14 June 1985 in a raid on the offices of the freedom fighters in Gaborone, Botswana's capital, killing 16 persons.

The apartheid regime also invaded Mozambique in the late seventies and early eighties. Zambia and Zimbabwe were also attacked and bombed by South Africa for supporting the freedom fighters.

Among those killed in Mozambique was Ruth First, the wife of anti-apartheid activist and commander of ANC guerrillas, Joe Slovo. She was killed on 17 August 1982 when she opened a parcel bomb addressed to her at the University of Eduardo Mondlane in Maputo, Mozambique's capital, where she worked as director of African studies.

One of the murders which fuelled the anti-apartheid struggle and led to more condemnation and further isolation of apartheid South Africa was that of Steve Biko, a black medical student and activist and leader of the Black Consciousness movement.

He was tortured and brutally beaten by the police and died in police custody after being transported naked, and tied, in the back of a police van for hundreds of miles.

He died in 1977 and became a powerful symbol for freedom. His name was invoked worldwide in the campaign against racial injustice and his death became a rallying cry for the liberation of South Africa from apartheid.

The struggle against apartheid was further galvanised, and took another turn, when a new constitution went into effect on 3 September 1984. It allowed nonwhites some representation but excluded blacks. The constitution stipulated that South Africa would have a tricameral parliament, with three houses of representation – one for whites, called the House of Assembly; one for Asians (who are mostly Indians), called the House of Delegates; and one for Coloureds, called the House of Representaitves.

But power was still in white hands. Only whites could make final decisions. And they had more seats in the new parliament than the Indians and Coloureds combined.

So, those were only cosmetic changes, and representation was more apparent than real.

Still, all that was enough to infuriate blacks. It meant that they didn't count at all, were not part of the equation, and would never be consulted on matters affecting their lives and the country as whole, unless fundamental change took place allowing them equal representation; which was totally out of the question as far as the regime was concerned during those years.

Adoption of the constitution triggered massive protests by blacks. More than 260 people were killed in racial violence between 1964 and 1985 as blacks protested, denouncing the new constitution and other apartheid policies.

In the worst incident in 25 years since the Sharpeville Massacre, police opened fire on black demonstrators near the manufacturing town of Uitenhage on 21 March 1985, killing 20. The government declared a state of emergency on July 20th and arrested scores of activists in an effort to end the violence.

But the struggle against apartheid continued. And as the struggle continued in the 1980s, the regime began to unravel.

Attacks against police stations and other government installations increased. And the government responded by imposing a state of emergency for an indefinite period. That was in 1985.

In 1986, Anglican Bishop Desmond Tutu addressed the United Nations and urged further actions against South Africa. Protests against apartheid continued with greater intensity. And in 1987, a wave of strikes and riots rocked the nation on the tenth anniversary of the Soweto uprising.

The apartheid regime was still strong, but the clock was ticking. And nothing could it turn it back. Even some of the staunchest supporters of apartheid knew that their days were numbered.

In 1989, President Botha was succeeded, first as party leader, then as president, by F.W. De Klerk. The change in leadership of the ruling party was a major transition. It also marked a change in the policies of the National Party towards nonwhites and signalled the beginning of the end of apartheid.

President de Klerk's government began to relax restrictions imposed by apartheid and, in February 1990, Nelson Mandela was finally freed after more than 27 years in prison. The African National Congress (ANC), which had been banned since 1960, was again legalized and Mandela became head of the ANC.

After Mandela was freed, he began to work with De Klerk in preparation for a transition to majority rule. But they had some differences, some profound, on how this goal was to be achieved.

Probably the biggest issue was de Klerk's – and his party's – contention that the National Party, hence whites in essence, should retain veto power over any legislation they did not agree with. Mandela and his colleagues refused to compromise on the matter. Allowing whites to have veto power would have rendered the transition to democracy meaningless.

In late 1991, the Convention for a Democratic South Africa (CODESA), a multiracial forum set up by de Klerk and Mandela, began working on plans for negotiations on a new constitution and a transition to a multiracial democracy under majority rule. And in March 1992, voters in a referendum open only to whites endorsed by a wide margin initiatives towards constitutional reform.

However, not everything went on smoothly. There were attempts by white extremists, including members of the ruling National Party, to derail the democratic process and the transition to black majority rule. Among the most bitter of opponents of the transition was former President Botha who even refused to attend Mandela's inauguration after Mandela was elected president of a democratic South Africa.

Other opponents of the transition included blacks, especially the Zulu who supported Chief Mangosuthu Buthelezi, leader of the predominantly Zulu Inkatha movement which he later converted into a political party, the Inkatha Freedom Party (IFP).

Buthelezi and his party were opposed to a strong central government supported by Mandela's African National Congress (ANC) and wanted South Africa to be a weak federal state under a federal constitution with extensive devolution of power to the provinces.

But Buthelezi was also opposed to the transition for other reasons. He did not want the ANC, the dominant anti-apartheid party, to assume power after the end of apartheid because it was not predominantly Zulu. The ANC was, instead, seen as a party that was dominated by the Xhosa and there were even jokes about it, saying the African National Congress was La Xhosa Nostra.

So, there were ethnic considerations, and rivalries, which also came into play during the transition period in spite of the fact that the ANC was not an ethnically-based party like the Zulu Inkatha Freedom Party but embraced members of all races and ethnic groups, although it is also true that the majority of the Xhosa were, indeed, supporters of the ANC, Mandela himself, a liberation icon, was Xhosa. So was Thabo Mbeki, who became his vice president, and other leading figures in the party.

But not all the top leaders of the ANC were Xhosa. They included Zulus such as Jacob Zuma, who years later served as vice president under Thabo Mbeki; Cyril Ramaphosa, a member of one of the small tribes, Frene Ginwala, an Indian, who became the first speaker of parliament of a democratic South Africa, and many others including whites.

That was not the case with the Inkatha Freedom Party of Mangosuthu Buthelezi. The party was solidly Zulu.

The supporters of the apartheid regime and other racists, as well as nonwhites who were opposed to the ANC for different reasons, took advantage of all this and exploited the differences and rivalries between the Zulu-based Inkatha movement and the African National Congress.

It became a virtual civil war between the two in which more than 10,000 people were killed. Given the scale of violence and the atrocities committed, it became obvious that there was a third force involved. And that was the apartheid regime itself. The Inkatha movement was supplied with weapons and South African security forces were actively involved in the conflict, supporting Buthelezi and his fellow Zulus in their war against the African National Congress.

All that was intended to stop the transition to black majority rule, and many blacks, especially in the Inkatha movement, became willing excutioners of their own people, fellow blacks, who were fighting for racial equality.

There were also reprisals by the supporters of the African National Congress and the Pan-Africanist Congress. And the government continued to rear its ugly head in these conflicts.

In September 1992, government-backed police forces fired on a crowd of ANC demonstrators in Ciskei, killing 28. And in April 1993, the secretary-general of the South African Communist Party (SACP), Chris Hani, was shot dead by a right-wing white extremist – an immigrant from Poland – who had conspired with a white conservative member of parliament to commit this dastardly act in an attempt to plunge the country into a racial civil war and derail the transition from apartheid to majority rule.

Chris Hani was the most popular black leader in South

Africa, after Nelson Mandela, and a potential president. It was widely believed that had Mandela not been around, Hani would probably have been the first president of a democratic South Africa.

In spite of all those setbacks, the transition to a new South Africa proceeded as planned. In 1993, an interim constitution was completed, ending nearly three centuries of white domination in South Africa. It also marked the end of white-minority rule on the African continent. Apartheid South Africa had been the last bastion of white supremacy on the continent, and the toughest one to demolish.

After the constitution was accepted, a multi-party transitional government council was formed with blacks in the majority. And in April 1994, days after the Inkatha Freedom Party ended an electoral boycott, multiracial democratic election's were held. They were the first in the nation's history, and the African National Congress won an overwhelming victory. Nelson Mandela became president of the new South Africa, a truly rainbow nation.

South Africa rejoined the Commonwealth in the same year apartheid rule ended after 33 years of absence. It also relinquished its last hold in Namibia, ceding the exclave of Walvis bay to Namibia.

The 1994 elections were some of the most democratic in the world, and South Africa's constitution one of the most democratic in history.

In 1994 and 1995, the last vestiges of apartheid were dismantled, and a new constitution was approved and adopted in May 1996.

The new consitution provided for a strong presidency under a federal state and eliminated provisions guaranteeing white-led and other minority parties representation in the government.

De Klerk and the National Party supported the new constitution in spite of the disagreements they had with the ANC on some of the provisions.

The Inkatha Freedom Party did not support the new constitution and its delegates, who had earlier walked out of the constitutional talks, did not participate in voting on the new constitution.

Shortly afterwards, de Klerk and the National Party left the government of national unity and became part of the opposition. After 1998, the National Party was renamed the New National Party to shed its image as a party for whites and the architect of apartheid.

Celebrating the end of white-minority rule was easy. Now the new government faced the daunting task of trying to address the inequities in society, a legacy of decades of apartheid and more than three hundred years of white domination It was a formidable challenge. And it is still one today more than a decade after the end of centuries of racial oppression and exploitation.

It will take generations before some of these problems are solved. And the wounds inflicted by apartheid may never heal.

In 1999, Thabo Mbeki, who served as vice president under Mandela and succeeded him as head of the ANC, led the party to a landslide victory and became president of South Africa.

The liberal Democratic Party became the leading opposition party. It united with the New National Party in 2000 to form the Democratic Alliance (DA). But the coalition did not last long. It ended towards the end of 2001 when the New National Party left the DA and formed a coalition with the ruling African National Congress (ANC).

And after its devastating electoral defeat in the parliamentary elections in April 2004, the New National Party merged with the African National Congress and voted to disband in April 2005.

Two of the most bitter enemies during the apartheid era had finally become one, united by a common cause and desire to serve South Africa as one nation and under a constitution which guarantees equality for all regardless of race. As the ANC's 1955 Freedom Charter stated, South Africa belongs to all those who live in it.

It is a collective sentiment shared across the nation, given concrete expression in the new South Africa.

And it is indeed a miracle that the party that started apartheid merged with the party that fought so hard to end apartheid and finally became one after apartheid ended.

Part II:

The Land

SOUTH AFRICA is a union of nine provinces. The current provincial structure was created after the end of apartheid when some of the former provinces, whose boundaries were drawn during the era of white minority rule, were divided to create more administrative units which became the new provinces.

There were four provinces before the end of apartheid: the Cape Province, Natal, Transvaal, and the Orange Free State.

We are going to look at each of the nine provinces in the new South Africa starting with the Free State.

Free State Province

The Free State was formerly known as the Orange Free State. Its current name is therefore simply a contraction of its original name.

The area of what came to be known as the Orange Free State was inhabited mostly by the Tswana in the early part of the 19th century. The Tswana still live in South Africa but many of them migrated north and settled in what came to be known as the British protectorate of Bechuanaland, what is Botswana today.

From the 1820s, Afrikaner farmers, people mostly of Dutch descent also known as Boers, moved into the Orange Free State – before it was named that – and their numbers increased after 1835 following a large migration known as the Great Trek. This large migration of Afrikaners into the region led to the establishment of a Dutch colony in the Orange Free State.

Established as a Boer state, it has throughout its history been a centre of Afrikaner culture and a monument to Afrikaner nationalism which eventually evolved into apartheid.

The Orange Free State became a self-sustaining colony and later an independent Boer republic in the 1850s. But it lost its independence in 1902 after the Dutch (Boers) were defeated by the British in the Boer War, also known as the South African War, of 1899 – 1902. It was the bloodiest conflict in the continent's colonial history up to that time and remains one of the most important events in the history of South Africa.

It later became a British colony and then a province of the Union of South Africa in 1910.

The capital of the Orange Free State (republic) was Bloemfontein. And it is still the capital of the Free State today in post-apartheid South Africa.

It was officially founded by the British in 1846 but Bloemfontein has historically been a predominantly Afrikaner town.

It was originally founded as a fort by the British army, built on dry grassland in an area inhabited by the Basotho, one of the African ethnic groups in South Africa. And in 1910, it became the judicial capital of South Africa. That was also the same year in which the Union of South Africa was founded.

The African National Congress (ANC), which led the struggle against apartheid until this abominable institution was abolished in the early 1990s, was also founded in Bloemfontein in 1912, only about two years after the Union of South Africa was formed by the British and the Dutch under British rule.

The city is located in central South Africa on the southern edge of the Highveld in a region of flat land, rolling plains and grassland and crop fields with some hills, hot summers and dry winters. The area also gets some snow.

And apart from being the judicial capital of South Africa, Bloemfontein also has many schools and private hospitals and is one of South Africa's most well-known cities. It is also the country's most central city where major routes intersect. The country's main national road which connects the provinces of Gauteng, the Western cape and the Eastern Cape, passes through the middle of th Free State. And the road network density of the province is the third-highest in the country.

Institutions of higher learning in Bloemfontein include the University of the Free State and the Central University of Technology.

Provincial boundaries were redrawn in 1994 when black homelands known as Bantustans – given nominal "independence" by the apartheid regime – were abolished and re-incorporated into the provinces of South Africa. One of the exceptions was the Orange Free State. Its boundaries remained the same.

The Free State Province is the third-largest province in South Africa with an area of 49,992 square miles.

It occupies about 10.6 per cent of the country's land area and is only slightly bigger than the Western Cape Province. But it has the second-smallest population and the second-lowest population density in the country.

The region has rich soil and a pleasant climate, making it highly productive in terms of agriculture. In fact, the Free State produces more than 70 per cent of grain in the entire country. It is the nation's granary and is known as South Africa's breadbasket.

Almost the entire province is at high elevation. It is mostly a plateau. Low areas are in the west at 4,000 feet above sea level. The elevation then rises gradually up to 6,000 feet in the east but there are higher points in the Drakensberg Mountains in the southeast.

The Free State also has a lot of minerals, including gold and diamonds, mostly in the northern and western parts of the province. In fact, the country's largest gold-mining complex is in the Free State. It is known as the Free State Consolidated Goldfields. And South Africa is, of course, the world's largest producer of gold. That shows how important the Free State is in gold production, not only in South Africa but in the entire world.

The Free State has 12 gold mines and produces 30 per cent of the nation's output, making the province the fifth-largest producer of gold in the world. And the only two gold refineries in South Africa, the Harmony Gold Refinery and the Rand Refinery, are located in the Free State.

Gold mines in the Free State are also a major source of silver in the country. And significant amounts of uranium found in the gold-bearing conglomerates of the gold fields are also extracted as a byproduct.

Bituminous coal is also mined in the province and converted to petrochemicals at Sasolburg. Oil refined from coal is one of South Africa's most important products and the country is leader on the continent in the conversion of coal to petroleum products.

The Free State also produces high-quality diamonds from its kimberlite pipes and fissures, and the country's largest deposit of bentonite is found in the Koppies district in the province.

There are other minerals found in the province in smaller quantities.

And although agriculture is major part of the economy in the Free State, the mining sector provides most of the jobs in the province. Still, the economy is mainly agricultural.

But the economy of the province has undergone major structural changes since 1989 even though agriculture and mining still remain the most important sectors of economic activity in this vibrant region of South Africa.

The economy has gradually shifted from dependence on the two primary sectors of mining and agriculture to an economy increasingly oriented towards manufacturing and export.

Synthetic rubber, pharmaceuticals, fertilisers, plastics, textiles and manufactured foods are among the products which constitute an important part of the province's economy which is becoming increasingly diversified.

About 14 per cent of the manufacturing in the province is classified as being in high-technology industries, the highest percentage among all provincial economies. And the chemicals sector in the northern part of the province is one of the most important in the southern hemisphere.

The Petrochemical company, Sasol, based in the town of Sasolburg, is a world leader in the production of fuels, waxes, chemicals and low-cost feedstock from coal. It is also a centre of innovation in the fuel sector.

But, in spite of the dominant role played by the mining sector in the provision of employment, there is no question that agriculture dominates the landscape of this fertile province. Farmland covers about 32,000 square kilometres, while 87,000 square kilometres are covered by natural veld and are also used grazing.

Agriculture in the province also plays a major role in high technology.

The Free State leads the nation in the production of biofuels, which is fuel from agricultural crops, and has a number of ethanol plants being built in the grain-producing areas of the western part of the province.

Crops contribute almost 66 per cent towards income in the agricultural sector of the province, while animal products account for about 30 per cent. The rest comes from horticulture.

Ninety percent of the cherries produced in South Africa come from the Ficksburg area in the eastern part of the Free State.

The Ficksburg district is also home to the country's two largest asparagus canning factories, and asparagus is the main vegetable crop in the province. Both varieties, green and white, are grown n the Free State.

Soya, sorghum, sunflowers and wheat are cultivated in the eastern Free State where farmers specialise in seed production. And about 40 per cent of the potatoes produced in South Africa come from some of the areas at high elevation in the province.

Maize is another important crop. Sheep, mainly for wool, cattle and chickens are also raised in the province, making animal husbandry and dairy farming an important economic activity.

Tobacco is also an important crop.

The province's floral industry flourishes on a contrast in seasons. The Free State's advantage in floriculture is the opposing seasons of the southern and northern hemispheres. The province exports about 1.2 million tons of cut flowers a year.

The province is also known for its varied climate. The eastern part of the province, whose topography or landscape is characterised by sandstone mountains, experiences frequent snowfalls, in remarkable contrast with the western part which sometimes gets extremely hot in the summer.

In general, summers can be described as warm to hot, and winters, cool to cold. The east is well-watered, while the west is much drier. Many parts in the west and in the south are also semi-desert.

Rain falls in the summer and the Free State Province can be extremely cold during winter months especially in the mountainous areas in the east.

In the capital Bloemfontein, hot, moist summers are common. Winters are cold and dry, sometimes with severe frost.

Besides Bloemfontein, the other major towns in the Free State Province include Bethlehem, which is known as the gateway to the Eastern Highlands of the province; Welkom, the heart of the mining industry dominated by gold; Odendaalsrus, another important gold-mining town; Kroonstad., an agricultural, administrative and educational centre; Sasolsburg, a town named after the petrochemical company Sasol; and Phuthaditjhaba, a vast, sprawling settlement known for its beautiful handcrafted items.

The Free State is bordered by six provinces: KwaZulu Natal on the east, Eastern Cape on the south, Northern cape on the west, North West Province on the northwest, Gauteng on the north, and by Mpumalanga Province on the northeast.

Located in the central eastern part of the country, the Free State Province also borders more districts in the small independent country of Lesotho and more provinces of South Africa than any other province. In fact, the Kingdom of Lesotho is virtually surrounded by the Free State Province.

Most of the people in the Free State Province are black Africans. They are mostly members of the Sotho ethnic group and speak Sesotho, the dominant language in the province. About 66 per cent of the people speak this language which is also the main language spoken in the neighbouring country of Lesotho.

Afrikaans, spoken mostly by whites of Dutch descent, is the dominant language in the ssouthwestern part of the province and in many major towns. It is also widely spoken in the provincial capital, Bloemfontein.

The Xhosa language, also known as isiXhosa, is spoken by some people in the province; so is Zulu, also known as isiZulu. Zulu is the main language spoken in Phumelela, a municipality in the eastern part of the Free State Province, while Setswana is the dominant language in Tokologo in the west.

They are among the nine officially recognised languages spoken by black South Africans who constitute about 80 per cent of the country's total population. Altogether, South Africa has eleven official languages. The other two are English and Afrikaans.

The Free State is also a major tourist attraction. Among its most attractive features is the largest visible meteor-impact site in the world. A beautiful range of hills in the northern part of the province is a part of this site. It has been declared by UNESCO as of one South Africa's seven World Heritage sites. And in the northeast is the Golden Gate Highlands National Park, another major tourist attraction.

And some of the world's highly treasured ancient rock paintings and other forms of art are found in the Free State. They are the work of the San, also known as Bushmen, a pejorative term. The San were the earliest inhabitants of South Africa and had lived in the region long before other Africans and Europeans migrated there, changing the demographic composition forever.

Many of the Afrikaner families in the Free State trace their ancestry to the Dutch settlers who moved into the region during the Great Trek in the 1830s and 1840s, an eastward and northeastward migration of about 12,000 Afrikaners from the Cape.

They are usually very conservative and are members of the Calvinist Dutch Reformed Church which was established in the country when the first Dutch settlers settled in the Cape in 1652.

North West Province

THE North West Province is one of the newest administrative regions in South Africa. It did not exist before, during white minority rule, and was created in 1994 after apartheid ended.

It is the sixth-largest province with an area of 44,911 square miles. It also ranks sixth in terms of population. In 2008, it had a population of about 3.4 million people.

It is located in north-west central South Africa and includes the northeastern part of the former Cape Province, the southeastern half of the former Transvaal Province, and most of the former Bantustan of Bophuthatswana.

It is bordered by the country of Botswana on the north and northwest, with a small part of its territory on the northeast also bordered by Botswana; and by the South African provinces of Limpopo on most of its northeastern part, Gauteng on the east, the Free State on the southeast, and by the Northern Cape Province on the southwest.

In the west is the Kalahari desert. The province is rich in minerals and is known as the Platinum Province.

The main language spoken in the province is Setswana which is also the same language spoken by most of the people, the Tswana, across the border in Botswana. Although the majority of the people belong to the Tswana ethnic group, there are members of other ethnic and racial groups who live in the province and speak their own languages as well. Other languages spoken include Afrikaans, isiXhosa, Sesotho, Xitsonga, Sepedi (which is Northern Sotho), isiZulu, isiNdebele, and English.

Besides black Africans who constitute the vast majority of the population – more than 90 per cent are black, of whom more than 65 per cent are Tswana - members of other racial groups who live in the North West Province include whites; members of mixed race who were officially known as Coloureds during apartheid; and Asians, mostly of Indian origin.

The most well-known city in the North West Province is Mafikeng, its capital.

The capital has an interesting history. Located on South Africa's border with Botswana, Mafikeng was once the headquarters of the Barolong, a clan of the Batswana people who are found on both sides of the border.

The town was founded by the British in the 1880s and was named Mafikeng, which in the Tswana language means 'place of stones." The town was built on an open veld by the banks of the upper Molopo River.

The British later changed the town's name to Mafeking, a slight variation in spelling to suit their pronunciation. The town is important in the history of South Africa because of the Jameson Raid. The raid, which started on 29 December 1895, was launched from Potlogo only 24 miles north of Mafeking and remains one of the most important events in the nation's history. It was a major cause of the Boer War.

The town came under siege when the Boer War broke out. The siege lasted for 217 days from October 1899 to May 1900 and made Robert Baden-Powell a national hero. A British army offier, he commanded the troops which defended Mafeking against the Boers and later founded the Boy Scout Movement.

Mafeking also once served as the capital of the British protectorate of Bechuanaland from 1894 until 1965 - just before Bechuanaland won independence from Britain - even though though it was not even a part of the protectorate but was on South African soil.

When Bechuanaland won independence on 30 September 1966 and changed its name to Botswana, it had already chosen Gaborone – within its territory – as its capital.

Located only 9 miles from the border with South Africa, Gaborone became the capital of Bechuanaland in

1965 as the country headed towards independence. And for many years, it was the fastest-growing city in the world, and with an excellent infrastructure.

Not long after Mafeking lost its unique and eminent status as the capital of a neighbouring country, Bechuanaland, it again became the capital of another "country," the Bantustan of Bophuthatswana in the 1970s before the adjoining town of Mmabatho was established as the capital of this black homeland.

In 1980, the original spelling of the town was restored and it again came to be known as Mafikeng. And after apartheid ended in 1994, Mafikeng and Mmabatho were merged and became the capital of the new North West Province.

And instead of chosing a new name for the capital, or using a hyphenated name, Mafikeng-Mmabatho following the merger of the two towns, the authorities simply decided to call the merged town, Mafikeng, and made it the capital of the new province in the new South Africa in the post-apartheid era.

The largest cities in the province are Potchefstroom and Klerksdorp. The other main towns are Brits and Rustenburg.

Rustenburg stands out in some fundamental respects among all the towns and cities in South Africa. Located about 70 miles north of Johannesburg, it is reportedly the fastest-growing city in South Africa. It also has the two largest platinum mines in the world and the world's largest platinum refinery which processes about 70 per cent of the world's platinum.

And although the city is heavily industrialised, it seems to have a rural landscape because it is green and lush, making it one of the major tourist attractions in the North West Province. And Sun City, another major tourist attraction, is only a few miles from Rustenburg.

Most of the province's economic activity is concentrated in the southern part between Potchefstroom and Klerksdorp, as well as Rustenburg and the eastern part of the province.

Besides its minerals, the province also has other natural resources. Major tourist attractions include Sun City, which is internationally renowned; the Pilanesberg National Park, the Madikwe Game Reserve and the Rustenburg Nature Reserve.

Sin City is one of the world's biggest entertainment centres, with world-class hotels, concert halls and theatres, beaches, casino, a meticulously reconstructed tropical rainforest and many other facilities in the most developed country on the entire African continent.

In terms of area, the North West Province is the fourth-smallest in the country, occupying 8.7 per cent of the country's total area. And it's mostly rural. Only 35 per cent of the people in the province live in towns and cities.

The land is mostly flat with scattered trees and grasslands, a topographical feature that can partly be explained in terms of the province's close proximity to the Kalahari desert.

The North West Province is also home to two world heritage sites: the Vredefort Dome, the world's largest visible meteor-impact crater, and the Taung hominid fossil site.

There are about 100 meteor-impact craters in the world and the one in South Africa is among the top three. It is also the oldest and largest clearly visible meteorite impact site on planet Earth.

The Taung hominid fossil site is one of the most important sites in the history of mankind and has been used, together with other findings including those in Tanzania, Kenya and Ethiopia and elsewhere in the world, in studying the history of man from the beginning.

The North West Province is a vast expanse of land in spite of its status as one of the smallest in the country. And because it is mostly rural, agriculture plays a major in the province's economic life.

In fact, the North West Province is sometimes referred to as the Texas of South Africa because of its many ranches. The province has some of the largest herds of cattle in the entire world, mostly at Stellaland near Vryburg. The Marico region is also known as cattle country.

And the areas around Brits and Rustenburg are fertile, mixed-crop land, enhancing the province's reputation as one of the nation's food baskets.

The province's reputation as a food basked is well-deserved, considering the large herds of cattle it has and which are a source of meat, as well as the fertile farmland in different part of the province. In fact, the North West Province is the biggest producer of white maize in the country, and its most important crops are maize and sunflowers.

Its economy is also heavily dependent on mineral production. Mining constitutes 23.3 percent of the province's economy.

The minerals mined in the province also make up 22.5 per cent of the entire mineral production in South Africa. And 94 per cent of South Africa's platinum is found in the North West Province. It is found in the Rustenburg and Brits districts which produce more platinum than any other single area in the entire world.

The North West Province also produces 25 percent of all the gold produced in South Africa. It is also a major source of granite, marble, fluorspar and diamonds.

And mining is a major source of employment in the province as much as it is in many other parts of South Africa.

What is known as the Platinum Corridor, extending from Pretoria in South Africa all the way to the eastern part of the neighbouring country of Botswana, provides more than a third of total employment in the North West Province.

Northern Cape Province

THE Northern Cape is one of the three provinces which once constituted the Cape Province.

The other two which were carved out of the Cape Province in 1994, together with the Northern Cape, were the Western Cape in the south and the Eastern Cape in the southeast.

Before it was divided into three separate provinces, the Cape Province was the largest province in South Africa.

It also has a special place in South African history as the region where Europeans established the first white settlement in the country. The first settlement was founded by the Dutch East India Company at the Cape in 1652.

It was also the only province where Coloureds had some voting rights during the apartheid era, although even these limited rights were severely curtailed by the apartheid regime in the 1960s and 1970s.

Coincidentally, what was once the largest province in South Africa during white minority rule also produced the largest province after the end of apartheid.

The Northern Cape is the largest province in South Africa with an area of 139,703 square miles. It is also sparsely populated, and distances between towns are enormous. It has the smallest population among all the provinces of South Africa.

In 2008, it had more than 1.1 million people and a population density of only three people per square kilometre in such a vast expanse of territory.

It constitutes almost an entire third - about 30.5% - of of South Africa's land area.

It is bordered by the countries of Botswana on the north and Namibia on the northwest; by the North West Province on the northeast, the Free State Province on the east, the Eastern Cape Province on the southeast, and by the

Western Cape Province on the south.

The Northern Cape Province is slightly larger than Germany and is well-known for its diamonds and as home to one of South Africa's most well-known cities, Kimberley, whose name - and history - is also associated with diamonds.

It lies to the south of its most important asset, the mighty Orange River, which feeds the agriculture and alluvial diamonds industries. The Orange River also forms the border with the country of Namibia in the north, while the Molopo River is at the border with Botswana to the northeast.

The Northern Cape Province is also famous for its spring flowers in the Namaqualand region in the western part of the province. It also has a shoreline in the west on the South Atlantic Ocean.

The northern part of the province is dominated mostly by the Kalahari Desert. Its landscape is also known for its vast arid plains with outcroppings of haphazard rock piles. The cold Atlantic Ocean forms the western boundary.

The Northern Cape is mostly arid and semi-arid and does not get much rain. And it can get extremely hot. But it can also get very cold in winter, especially in the southern part of the province when it snows.

The province gets winter rainfall in a narrow strip of land along the coast and very little little in summer.

Vegetation is of low shrubland and grass, and trees limited to water courses.

Although the Northern Cape Province is known for its diamonds, it is also known for its fertile land around the Orange River which includes most of South Africa's sultana vineyards.

The Northern Cape is enjoying a tremendous growth in value-added activities, including game-farming. Food production and processing for the local and export market is also growing significantly.

Underpinning the growth and development plan of the

province are the investment projects that link up with the existing plans of the Namaqua Development Corridor. The focus is on the export of sea products and others.

The economy of a large part of the Northern Cape, the interior Karoo, depends on sheep-farming, while the karakul-pelt industry is one of the most important in the Gordonia district of Upington.

The province has fertile agricultural land. In the Orange River Valley, especially at Upington, Kakamas and Keimoes, grapes and fruit are cultivated intensively. Wheat, fruit, peanuts, maize and cotton are produced at the Vaalharts Irrigation Scheme near Warrenton.

But its agricultural sector is small compared with mining. And there is no question that the Northern Cape is rich in minerals and is known worldwide for that. The country's major diamond pipes are found in the Kimberley district. Alluvial diamonds are found on the opposite, western, side of the province, washed westwards by the Orange River into the Atlantic Ocean, where they are extracted from the beaches and sea between Alexander Bay and Port Nolloth.

Until recently, the majority of small- to medium-scale alluvial operations were concentrated along or near the Vaal River system in the east. With the rapidly depleting deposits available for mining, there has been a gradual shift towards the Orange River system.

The Sishen Mine near Kathu is the biggest source of iron ore in South Africa, while the copper mine at Okiep is one of the oldest mines in the country. Copper is also mined at Springbok and Aggenys.

Other minerals found here are asbestos, manganese, fluorspar, semi-precious stones and marble.

The Northern Cape Province also has the dubious distinction of being the place where some racist Afrikaners made their last stand against the wave of multiracial democracy that swept across the country in the early 1990s to end apartheid.

They were determined to preserve their old ways and maintain apartheid and founded a whites-only racist settlement called Orania.

Orania was intended to be the nucleus of an independent state for Afrikaners but only a few of them were attracted to this racist outpost. They knew they could not turn back the tide of history. Apartheid was over.

It is also in the Northern Cape Province where another interesting footnote to history was added.

The province - when it was still a part of the Cape Province - became the home of more than 1,000 members of the San tribe who emigrated from Namibia after that country won independence in 1990 from the South African apartheid regime which ruled Namibia (South West Africa) virtually as an integral part of South Africa.

When Namibia was fighting for independence from South Africa, the San worked for the apartheid regime as trackers and scouts, helping the South African government to track down the Namibian freedom fighters of the South West African People's Organisation (SWAPO).

Fearing reprisals after SWAPO came to power in Namibia, the San who had worked in Namibia for the apartheid regime sought sanctuary in South Africa and were allowed to settle in the northern part of what was then the Cape Province, the part which is now the Northern Cape Province.

The largest city in the Northern Cape is Kimberley. Located on the province's eastern border, it is also the provincial capital.

Other important towns are Upington, centre of the karakul sheep and dried fruit industries, and the most northerly wine-making region of South Africa; Springbok, in the heart of the Namaqualand spring flower country; Kuruman, founded by the Scottish missionary Robert Moffat; and De Aar, hub of the South African railway network.

Sutherland is the site of the southern hemisphere's

largest astronomical observatory, the multinational-sponsored Southern African Large Telescope, or SALT, Africa's eye on the universe.

The area where Kimberly was built was the site of the diamond rush in the region when thousands of people flocked into the area in search of diamonds after initial spectacular findings of diamond pebbles triggered the rush of diamond seekers.

The town was first named New Rush but was later renamed Kimberley in June 1873 in honour of the British Secretary of State for the Colonies at the time, John Woodhouse, 1st Earl of Kimberley.

The British were, during that period, in control of much of South Africa and quickly annexed the diamond-mining area, to the consternation of the Boers who wanted it to be incorporated into their colony, the Orange Free State.

Kimberley grew very fast and became the largest city in the area.

Its phenomenal growth was attributed to a massive migration of Africans from different parts of the continent – especially from the countries of East and Southern-Central Africa – who wanted to work in the mines. And they found employment right away because of the cheap labour they provided to De Beers, the company which operated the mines.

Kimberley again gained prominence in history when in September 1882 – only a few years after its founding – it became the first town in the southern hemisphere to install electric street lighting. It was also in Kimberley where the first school of mines in South Africa was established in 1896.

The school was later relocated to Johannesburg where it became the founding institution of the University of the Witwatersrand, the foremost academic institution for English speakers in South Africa unto this day.

The first aviation school in South Africa was also founded in Kimberley in 1913. It started training pilots of the South African Aviation Corps, and later the South African Air Force.

The first stock exchange in South Africa was also opened in Kimberley, the city of diamonds.

Probably more than anything else besides the diamond mining regions of Kimberley and Alexander Bay, the city or town of Kimberley has played a major role in thrusting the Northern Cape Province into the spotlight.

The province is also known for many other attractions including the Kalahari Gemsbok National Park which is part of a trans-frontier park that extends into Botswana. Three-quarters of the park lies in Botswana and one-quarter in South Africa.

The Kgalagadi Transfrontier Park, Africa's first cross-border game park, joins South Africa's Kalahari Gemsbok National Park to the Gemsbok National Park in Botswana. It is one of the largest conservation areas in southern Africa, and one of the largest remaining protected natural ecosystems in the world. The park provides unfenced access to a variety of game between South Africa and Botswana.

The Ai-Ais-Richtersveld Transfrontier Conservation Park spans the border with Namibia, with some of the most spectacular scenery of the arid and desert environments in southern Africa.

Bisected by the Orange River, it comprises the Ai-Ais Hot Springs Game Park in Namibia, and the Richtersveld National Park in South Africa. Distinctive features include the Fish River Canyon - often likened to the Grand Canyon in the US - and the Ai-Ais hot springs.

The Namaqualand region in the western part of the province is famous for its Namaqualand daisies. In fact, the area is known worldwide its spectacular annual explosion of spring flowers which, for a short period every year, attracts thousands of tourists.

The Orange River is one of Africa's main rivers. It flows through the Northern Cape Province. The river forms a boundary between the Northern Cape and the Free State provinces on the southeast; and between the Northern Cape and Namibia on the northwest.

The Orange River is a major source of irrigation not only in the Northern Cape Province but also in other parts of South Africa. But it assumes special significance in the Northern Cape because this is a dry region where it is used to irrigate many vineyards near Upington. And its water is used in other parts of the province.

Nowhere is the Orange River more impressive than at the Augrabies Falls, which ranks among the world's greatest cataracts on a major river. The 19 separate falls cascade over a granite plateau, dropping a total of 191 metres to a 43-metre-deep pool gouged out by the force of the water.

In terms of demographics, the Northern Cape Province has - more than any other province - the largest number of people who are native speakers of Afrikaans. They are mostly Afrikaners and people of mixed race once officially known as Coloureds.

Afrikaans is the most widely spoken language in the Northern Cape. About 70 percent of the people speak Afrikaans, 20 per cent speak Tswana, and about 6.5 per cent speak Xhosa.

Coloureds constitute about 52 per cent of the population; blacks, mostly Tswana, about 36 per cent; whites, about 12 per cent, and Asians (mostly of Indian origin), less than half a per cent.

The last remaining true San people - so-called Bushmen - live in the Kalahari area of the Northern Cape. The area, especially along the Orange and Vaal rivers, is rich in San rock engravings. A good collection of San artifacts can be seen at the McGregor Museum in Kimberley. The province is also rich in fossils.

And, in spite of its vast expanse of territory, the Northern Cape is not only the least populated province in South Africa; it is also one of the least populated regions on the entire African continent.

Western Cape Province

THE Western Cape Province is the fourth-largest province in South Africa with an area of 49,950 square miles. And it ranks fifth in terms of population. In 2008, it had a population of more than 4.8 million people.

It is bordered on the north by the Northern Cape Province, on the east by theEastern Cape Province, on the south by the Indian Ocean, and on the west by the Atlantic Ocean.

The sub-Antarctic dependency of the Prince Edwards islands is under the jurisdiction of the Western Cape Province. The Breede and Berg Rivers are major rivers of the province.

The Western Cape is known for its stunning beauty, with a magnificent geographical landscape of mountains and very fertile valleys.

Its mountain ranges average in height from 1,000 metres to 2,300 metres. The far interior forms part of the Karoo Basin and is generally arid and hilly with a sharp escarpment in the north. Coastal areas range from sandy between capes, to rocky to steep and mountainous in different places. A temperate southern coastline is fringed with mountains.

The Western Cape Province is also the southernmost region of the African continent with Cape Agulhas as its southernmost point.

It is known for its vegetation which is extremely diverse and has one of the world's seven floral kingdoms almost exclusively endemic to the province. The floral kingdom, known as the Cape Floral Kingdom, contains more plant species than the whole of Europe.

The kingdom is one of the Western Cape's two

UNESCO World Heritage Sites, places of "outstanding value to humanity."

The other one is Robben Island in Table Bay near Cape Town, used for centuries as a prison for dissidents and outcasts. Now an essential stop for visitors to the region, it was on this island that Nelson Mandela spent the bulk of his 27 years in prison.

Robben Island also is one of the country's seven World Heritage sites. It was declared a World Heritage Site in 1999 and is home to the Robben Island Museum featuring a lot of material on those who were imprisoned there during the struggle against apartheid, and much more.

The Western Cape Province also is extremely rich in species diversity. It has more plant species on the Table Mountain than the entire United Kingdom (UK) has. The landscape is also covered or dotted with various types of shrubs, thousands of flowering plant species and some small trees.

The arid interior is dominated by Karoo drought-resistant shrubbery. The West Coast and Little Karoo are semi-arid regions and are typified by many species of succulents and drought-resistant shrubs and acacia trees. The Garden Route is extremely lush, with temperate rainforest covering many areas adjacent to the coast and along the mountain ranges. Typical species are hardwoods of majestic height. They include Yellowwood, Stinkwood and Ironwood trees.

The region around Knysna and Tsitsikamma has the country's largest indigenous forests, a fairyland of ancient tree giants, ferns and abundant birdlife.

Products of the forests include sought-after furniture made from the indigenous yellowwood, stinkwood and white pear trees.

The province's climate has earned the region distinction as a tourist paradise. Most of the province has what is considered to be a Mediterranean-type of climate with cool, wet winters and warm, dry summers.

The province's typographical features and the influence of ocean currents from the warm waters of the Indian Ocean and the cold waters of the Atlantic have played a major role in influencing the climate.

Two oceans meet on the coast of the Western Cape: the cold Atlantic Ocean is in the west, while the warmer Indian Ocean lies on the southern coast. The plankton-rich cold Benguela current flows along the west coast and is considered to be one of the richest fishing grounds in the entire world.

The interior wide-open landscape of Karoo has a semi-arid climate with cold, frosty winters and hot summers with some thunderstorms now and then. In fact, thunderstorms are rare in the Western cape Province except in the Karoo interior.

The Garden Route and the Overberg on the southern coast have a maritime climate with cool, moist winters and mild, moist summers. And Mossel Bay in the Garden Route is considered to have the second mildest climate in the world surpassed only by Hawaii.

But there are extreme temperatures inland where it gets very hot and very cold. However, in areas near the coast, such extreme temperatures are rare. The west coast is extremely dry.

Snow is common in winter in areas of high altitude. But frost is relatively rare in coastal areas and in the valleys which support abundant agriculture.

The only part of the province which has low temperatures throughout the year is the dependency of the Prince Edwards Islands. They have cool to cold temperatures . They also experience high precipitation because of their geographical location and surroundings influenced by the cold Atlantic Ocean.

The province had a population of almost 5 million in 2008 and ranked fifth in the nation. It constitutes about 10.6 percent of the country's total area and is the fourth-largest province, only slightly smaller than the Free State.

It is roughly the size of England or Greece; also about the same size as the southern state of Louisiana in the United States.

A confluence of diverse cultures has given the province a cosmopolitan character, creating a demographic profile quite different from the national pattern.

Centuries of trade and immigration have created a population with genetic and linguistic links to different parts of Europe, southeast Asia, India and Africa, making the province truly international.

The majority of the people are Coloureds who constitute about 54 per cent of the province's population. Blacks, who are mostly Xhosa, make up about 27 percent per cent, whites about 18 per cent, and people of Asian origin about 1 per cent.

Afrikaans is the main language spoken mostly by Coloureds. About 55 per cent of the people, including many whites as well as a significant number of blacks, speak the language. Xhosa is spoken by about 24 per cent of the people, and English by about 19 per cent.

Other languages spoken, although in smaller numbers, include Zulu, Sotho, Tswana, Swati, Venda and Tsonga. They are all black African languages.

Located in south-west Africa, the Western Cape was part of the Cape Province, then the largest province in the country.. Before the Union of South Africa was formed in 1910, what became the Cape Province was known as the Cape Colony.

In 1994, after apartheid formally ended, the Cape Province was split up into three provinces: Western Cape, Northern Cape, and Eastern Cape which includes the former Xhosa homelands of Transkei and Ciskei.

Although the African National Congress (ANC) which led the struggle against apartheid became the ruling party at the national level and in most of the provinces, it did not have equal success in the Western Cape.

Soon after apartheid ended, the Western Cape stood out

as one of only two provinces where the African National Congress lost elections. The voters, who were and still are mostly Coloured, voted for the National Party – which instituted apartheid – to rule the province.

The other province which rejected the ANC mandate was KwaZulu Natal where the people overwhelmingly voted for the Zulu-dominated Inkatha Freedom Party (IFP) to be the ruling party in this overwhelmingly Zulu province.

The capital of the Cape Province is Cape Town, one of the most well-known cities in the world and a major international tourist attraction.

The other major cities are Stellenbosch, Worcester, Paarl, and George. The Garden Route and Overberg are popular coastal tourism areas.

But among all the cities in the province, it is Cape Town which stands out, not only because it is the provincial capital but also because of its prominent role in the history of the country and in contemporary times because of its status as a cosmopolitan city of international stature.

It is the second most populous city in South Africa and had a population of about three-and-a-half million people in 2008. It is also the nation's legislative capita where the National Parliament is located. Many government offices are also located in Cape Town.

Cape Town is famous for its harbour and natural setting which includes the spectacular Table Mountain and Cape Point. And because of its geographical landscape, it is considered to be one of the most beautiful cities in the entire world.

It was originally established as as a replenishment or supply station for ships passing the treacherous coast around the Cape on long voyages between the Netherlands and the Dutch East Indies. The Portuguese also used it as a station on their way to East Africa – what is now Mozambique, Tanzania and Kenya – and India where they established settlements. It w as established more than 200 years before the construction of the Suez Canal in 1869 which shortened the distance between Europe and Asia as well as East Africa.

The Dutch arrived at the Cape on 6 April 1652 and went on to establish the first European settlement in South Africa. Cape Town grew from a mere supply station - for ships going round the Cape and bound for East Africa and Asia - to a major European settlement, mostly Dutch. It eventually became a major urban centre and was the largest city in South Africa until the growth of Johannesburg.

During its early years when it was a way-station for ships going to the Dutch East Indies, it grew slowly and experienced labour shortage, prompting the settlers to bring slaves from Indonesia and Madagascar. Many of these slaves became the ancestors of the first Cape Coloured communities. The Dutch also, through intermarriage with the members of the Asian and African communities at the Cape also contributed to the growth of the Coloured population.

Cape Town has another outstanding feature. It occupies a large area of about 950 a square miles and is the largest city in South Africa in terms of territorial size. And because of that, it has a lower population density than other South African cities.

Cape Town also occupies a unique place in the struggle against apartheid. Most of the main leaders, including Nelson Mandela, Walter Sisulu and Govan Mbeki, were imprisoned near Cape Town on Robben Island which only 12 kilometers offshore from the city. And when Mandela got out of prison after serving 27 ½ years, he made his first speech in decades on 11 February 1990 from the balcony of Cape Town Hall just hours after being released.

The city of Cape Town also plays a major role in the country's economic growth. Since the end of apartheid in 1994, it has enjoyed phenomenal economic growth which is attributed to a boom in tourism and real estate development. More than 1.5 million tourists visit Cape Town every year.

It is a major commercial and industrial centre. The largest media company in Africa, Naspers, is in Cape Town. The city is also known for its academic institutions including the internationally renowned University of Cape Town. Another institution of higher learning of international stature, Stellenbosch University, is located 50 kilometres from the city.

Cape Town also is known for its architectural heritage. It has the highest density of Cape Dutch style buildings in the world; a style which combines the architectural traditions of the Netherlands, Germany and France.

The cosmopolitan character of Cape Town was tarnished in May 2008 when more than 20,000 black African immigrants were uprooted and displaced in violent xenophobic attacks by black South Africans who accused the immigrants of taking their jobs – and even their women – forcing many of them to return to their countries. Even those who remained in Cape Town and other parts of the province continued to live in fear.

The wave of terror swept across the nation during the same period and was the worst form of violence the country experienced since the end of apartheid.

But the province's reputation as a prosperous region remained virtually intact.

In fact, the Western Cape Province is one of the richest in South Africa. Its gross domestic product (GDP) ranks third in the nation, contributing about 14.5% to the nation's total.

The largest industry is textile manufacturing but other industries are growing fast. They include high technology, television production and advertising.

The financial sector has also witnessed phenomenal growth and contributes significantly to the province's economic prosperity. In fact, many of South Africa's major insurance companies and banks are based in the Western Cape. Also most of the country's petroleum companies and the largest segment of the printing and publishing industry are found in Cape Town.

The Western Cape Province has, in terms of output, the third-largest manufacturing sector in the country, surpassed only by those in Gauteng and KwaZulu-Natal provinces. But the clothing and textile industry remains the biggest source of employment in the province in the industrial sector.

Although it is an integral part of the most underdeveloped part of the world, Africa, there's no question that the Western Cape Province has facilities that are comparable to the best in the West and in other highly industrialised regions round the globe. It has excellent hospitals, schools, roads and highways as well as telecommunications facilities.

Among all the provinces in South Africa, Western Cape has the highest percentage of educated people and a labour force of very high skills, in sharp contrast with most parts of the continent.

And it has through the years been a powerful magnet drawing immigrants from all over Africa until the xenophobic attacks of May 2008 which forced tens of thousands of these immigrants to leave South Africa and discouraged others from going to the land of "milk and honey."

The Western Cape Province is also one of the most beautiful regions on the African continent and in the entire world, as demonstrated by the very large number of tourists who flock to this parts of South Africa. It attracts the largest number of foreign visitors among all the provinces.

Many of them decide to stay. They include African tourists. In fact, visitors from other parts of Africa constitute a large percentage of the tourists who visit the Western Cape Province.

The province is also known for its agricultural prosperity. The Mediterranean climate of the peninsula, and the mountainous region beyond it, is excellent for grape cultivation, with a number of vineyards producing excellent wines.

Other fruit and vegetables are also grown in that region, and wheat is an important crop to the north and east of Cape Town.

The southern coastal area is also fertile and ideal for agriculture, while fishing is the most important industry along the west coast. Sheep farming is the mainstay of the Karoo, and other forms of husbandry take place in the better watered parts of the province.

The sheltered valleys between mountains are ideal for the cultivation of export-grade fruit such as apples, table grapes, olives, peaches and oranges. And a variety of vegetables is cultivated in the eastern part of the Western Cape, while the wheat-growing Swartland and Overberg districts are the country's breadbasket.

The inland Karoo region and the Overberg district around Bredasdorp produce wool and mutton, as well as pedigree Merino breeding stock.

Other animal products include broiler chickens, eggs, dairy products, beef and pork.

Also, the Western Cape is the only province with an outlet for the export of horses, earning millions in foreign revenue.

The province is also a leader in the export of ostrich meat to Europe. In addition to meat, fine leatherware and ostrich feathers are also exported to destinations all over the world.

The Western Cape Province is a region whose economic activities span the entire spectrum. And it is a hub of the South African economy without which South African wouldn't be what it is today.

Eastern Cape Province

THE Eastern Cape Province was created in 1994 after the end of apartheid. It consists of the former homelands of the Transkei and Ciskei, and the eastern portion of the former Cape Province.

It is the second-largest province in terms of area, after the Northern Cape, and the third largest in terms of population. It had a population of about 7 million people in 2008 and is roughly the size of the South American country of Uruguay in terms of area. It has an area of 65,475 square miles and constitutes almost 14 per cent of South Africa's land area.

The Eastern Cape Province is the traditional home of the Xhosa, the country's second largest ethnic group after the Zulu. And it stands out among all South Africa's provinces as the birthplace of many prominent figures in the nation's history and in the struggle against apartheid. They include Nelson Mandela, Walter Sisulu, Govan Mbeki, Oliver Tambo, Thabo Mbeki, Desmond Tutu, Winnie Madikizela-Mandela, and Steve Biko, among others.

The Xhosa constitute the vast majority of the population in the province, more than 80 per cent; Coloureds, about 7.5 per cent; whites, about 5 per cent, and those of Asian origin, less than half a per cent.

The main language is Xhosa. Afrikaans is spoken by about 9.5 per cent of the people, and English by almost 4 per cent of the province's population. Many black Africans also speak Afrikaans and English as they do in other parts of South Africa.

The province is on the southeastern coast of South Africa, along the Indian Ocean. It is also known for its cliffs and rough seas as well as dense green bush in an area known as the Wild Coast, a term reminiscent of the Wild West in American history although used in a different context. The Wild Coast is also known to be a graveyard for many vessels.

The Eastern Cape is bordered by the Western Cape Province on the west and southwest; the Northern Cape on the northwest, the Free State on the north and a part of the northwest; by the country of Lesotho on the north and northeast, Kwazulu-Natal Province also on the far northeast, and by the Indian Ocean on the east.

The western part of the province is mostly dry and semi-arid, dominated by the Karoo, a semi-desert region, except in the far south where there is a temperate rain forest.

Most of the province is hilly and mountainous. Even the coast is generally rugged although interspersed with beaches. And the eastern part of the province from East London towards the border with KwaZulu-Natal Province is lush grassland with intermittent forest. This is the Transkei, a region of rolling hills punctuated by deep gorges. And as you go from the west towards the east, it gets wetter and wetter.

The province has remarkable contrasts in its climate. It has frosty winters and hot summers. And some parts of the province such as Grahamstown have mild temperatures. And you go farther east, you see more rain and more rain, also an increase in humidity. And the climate becomes more subtropical along the coast with summer rainfall. But the interior can get very cold during winter, sometimes with a considerable amount of snow in the mountainous regions.

The diversity of the province's landscape is best demonstrated by the contrast between the western interior which is mainly arid, dominated by the Karoo semi-desert region, and the east which is well-watered and green. The east also has a long coastline of about 500 miles with very good beaches; it's also known for its national parks with a wide range of animals including elephants, buffalo and the rare black rhino.

The long curve of coastline, large area and the considerable east-west and north-south distances it covers give the province extremely varied vegetation.

There are various floral habitats in different parts of the province and along the coast, the northern tropical forests intermingle with the more temperate woods of the south.

Rolling grasslands dominate the eastern interior of the province, while the western central plateau is savanna bushveld. The northern inland is home to the aromatic, succulent-rich Karoo habitat.

Eastern Cape Province also has the only ski resort in South Africa on the slopes of the highest peak in the province in the Southern Drakensberg mountains. It also has one of the country's most popular inland resorts famous for its hot springs. There resort is located on an agricultural plateau on the Orange River.

The Eastern Cape is one of the poorest provinces in South Africa but with a lot of potential to achieve economic growth. It also has some parts which are ideal for agriculture including the fertile Langkloof, known for its rich apple harvests

Tourism is one of its main assets, and the coast is its bggest attraction. Many people are attracted by its great beaches.

They are also attracted by its game parks and the province's spectacular landscape characterised by hills, mountains and valleys as well as forests. Also, Africa's largest arts festival, South Africa's National Arts Festival, is held in Grahamstown every year for 11 days. Grahamstown is also known as the City of Saints because of its 52 churches.

Other important sectors of the economy include include finance, real estate, business services, wholesale and retail trade, and hotels and restaurants.

As in most parts of South Africa, agriculture constitutes the backbone of the province's economy. And the largest number of people involved in economic activities work in agriculture.

The province has a lot of fertile land enabling it to produce a variety of commodities in the agricultural sector. For example, the fertile Langkloof Valley in the southwest has enormous deciduous fruit orchards, while the Karoo is known for its sheep.

The Alexandria-Grahamstown area produces pineapples, chicory and dairy products, while coffee and tea are cultivated at Magwa.

People in the former Transkei region are dependent on cattle, maize and sorghum-farming more than anything else.

And plans are underway to grow olives in the Eastern Cape. Fort Hare University has played a prominent role in developing an olive nursery for this purpose in collaboration with other parties.

Forestry also is expected to play a bigger role in the province's economic growth. And as a coastal region, the Eastern Cape Province is actively involved in the fishing industry which plays a significant role in the province's economy.

In spite of the province's poverty, whose economy is dominated by subsistence agriculture, the Eastern Cape has two major industrial centres, Port Elizabeth and East London, where cars and other vehicles are made. Some of the world's biggest car manufacturers, General Motors and Volkswagen, have assembly plants in the Port Elizabeth area. And Daimler-Chrysler has a large plant in East London.

In 2008, one of the biggest construction projects was going on at Coega, about 12 miles north of Port Elizabeth, where a new harbour is being built. Once completed, the harbour is expected to play a major role in the province's economic development.

In fact, the status of Port Elizabeth as a major harbour or seaport is also demonstrated by the fact that it has the most significant ore loading facilities in the entire southern hemisphere.

The province's capital is Bhisho which once served as the capital of the bantustan or homeland of Ciskei.

Port Elizabeth is the largest city in the Eastern Cape Province and one of the largest in the country. It is also known as Madiba Bay; Madiba is Nelson Mandela's nickname.

The city also is one of the major sea ports in South Africa and on the African continent. And it constitutes the biggest part of the Nelson Mandela Metropolitan Municipality - also known as the Nelson Mandela Bay Municipality - which had a population of more than one million people in 2008.

The metropolitan area also includes the neighbouring towns of Uitenhage and Despatch and agricultural areas around it. The name of the municipality was chosen to honour Nelson Mandela.

Port Elizabeth also is the centre of South Africa's motor vehicle industry. Besides General Motors and Daimler-Volkswagen which have plants in Port Elizabeth and Uitenhage, many other automotive companies are also have plants and offices in Port Elizabeth. They include Ford and Continental Tyres.

And most industries in the Port Elizabeth metropolitan area are geared towards the motor vehicle industry.

The other large city in Eastern Cape Province is East London. It is the second-largest after Port Elizabeth. It is also one of South Africa's most well-known cities. It also enjoys distinction as the country's only river port.

The city itself had a population of about 250,000 people, and the metropolitan area, 700,000, in 2008.

Another prominent town in the Eastern Cape Province is Grahamstown which is also home to Rhodes University, one of South Africa's main academic institutions. It was the first town to be built by the British in South Africa.

The Eastern Cape Province also stands out in the

history of South Africa as the place where the British, the Xhosa and the Afrikaners first made contact more than 200 years ago.

It was also in the Eastern Cape where the Xhosa fought the white man for 100 years to maintain their independence their way of life. A total of nine wars were fought between 1779 and 1878.

The region is also known as Frontier Country because of its role in South African history and as a site where a clash of civilisations – between Africa and Europe – took place in one of the most important events which shaped the country's future for generations. Had the Xhosa won the war against the Europeans – the British and the Afrikaners – the history of the South Africa would have taken an entirely turn.

The most famous battle took place around Grahamstown in 1819 and the Xhosa, under the leadership of Nxele – also known as Makana – almost won until the British turned back the tide with superior firepower.

It has been described by some observers as the most significant battle in the history of South Africa probably because of its potential to change the course of South Africa history.

Had the British been routed, they may not have attempted to reconquer the Xhosa or pursue their imperial ambitions elsewhere in South Africa. And the destruction of Grahamstown by the Xhosa would have had great symbolic significance since this was the first town the British built in South Africa. The loss by the British would have had a devastating impact on British morale, while boosting the spirits of the Xhosa.

Today the battle area is known as Egazini in Xhosa, meaning the "Place of Blood," and a monument to the Xhosa warriors who died in that conflict – as well as in other wars in defence of their motherland – was built at the site to honour them.

As a result of the battle at Grahamstown, the British

decided to establish a permanent settlement with 4,000 British inhabitants to consolidate their control over the territory. And as the history of South Africa shows, the British had great success in extending and consolidating their control over the country and way out proportion to their limited numbers compared to the indigenous people. After the arrival of the British settlers, Grahamstown grew rapidly and became the second-largest town in South Africa after Cape Town.

The Eastern Cape Province is also significant in another respect on a continental scale. It is home to Fort Hare University - in the small town of Alice - a black institution of higher learning, which attracted students from many parts of Africa.

Among its alumni are many leaders including Nelson Mandela, Oliver Tambo, Govan Mbeki, all of them South African leaders; and Seretse Khama as well as Robert Mugabe both of whom years later became presidents of their respective countries after the end of colonial rule. Seretse Khama became president of Botswana, and Robert Mugabe, of Zimbabwe, to name only a few of the many prominent Africans who went through Fort Hare.

KwaZulu-Natal Province

BEFORE the end of apartheid, most of what is KwaZulu-Natal Province today was simply known as Natal.

The name Natal comes from Portuguese. Portuguese explorer Vasco da Gama, on his way to India, landed on the KwaZulu coastline on Christmas day in 1497 and named the area "Natalia," which means Christmas in Portuguese. When the British took over the region from the Boers – it was once a Boer Republic called Natalia – they renamed it Natal.

The Zulu also had a homeland called KwaZulu during

the era white minority rule. After apartheid ended, the province of Natal and the bantustan of KwaZulu merged to form KwaZulu-Natal Province. The province also is the native land of the Zulu, South Africa's largest ethnic group.

It is also the only province in South Africa which includes the name of its dominant ethnic group in its name.

Located in the southeastern part of the country, KwaZulu-Natal Province is bordered by three other South African provinces – Mpumalanga on the north, Free State on the west, and Eastern Cape on the southwest - and by the countries of Lesotho in some parts on the southwest, Swaziland on the northeast, and by Mozambique on the far northeast. And on the east, it is bordered by the Indian Ocean.

It is the largest province in South Africa in terms of population and ranks seventh in terms of area. In 2008, it had a population of more than 10 million people, bigger than that of many countries on the continent. It is roughly the size of Portugal and is the country's third-smallest province occupying about 7.7 per cent of South Africa's land area. It has an area of 35,560 square miles.

More than 85 per cent of population of KwaZulu-Natal Province is black African. South Africans of Asian descent, mostly Indian, constitute about 8.5 percent of the population; whites, about 4.7 percent, and Coloureds, about 1.5 per cent.

Zulu is spoken by 80.6 per cent of the people in the province; English by 13.6 per cent, Xhosa by 2.3 per cent, and Afrikaans by 1.5 per cent.

KwaZulu-Natal also has a very interesting history as a battleground between the Zulu and the Europeans who conquered South Africa. One of the bloodiest conflicts in African colonial history was the Battle of Isandhlawana in January 1879 in Zululand. The British lost. It was a humiliating defeat and the first loss the British suffered since the Crimean War.

KwaZulu-Natal Province has distinct geographical features which provide remarkable contrasts for this part of southeastern Africa. Along the coast of the Indian ocean is a lowland region which is very narrow in the south but gets wider in the northern part of the province.

In the central part of the province is the Natal Midlands, an undulating hilly plateau that rises towards the west. The province also has two mountainous areas: the Drakensberg Mountains in the west and the Lebombo Mountains in the north.

Also known as the garden province of South Africa, KwaZulu-Natal is a subtropical region of lush and well-watered valleys, washed by the warm Indian Ocean. It is also one of the country's most popular tourist destinations. One of the areas which is one of the province's biggest tourism assets is the Drakensberg mountain range with several peaks which exceed 9,000 feet. Some are almost 10,000 feet.

The Drakensberg Mountains are recognised as a World Heritage Site because of their magnificent beauty and the rock art found in their caves. The art was done by the San – also sometimes disparagingly called Bushmen – and is the richest concentration of such art on the entire African continent.

Between the mountains and the humid, subtropical coastline is savannah grassland. This is the midlands region, known as the Natal Midlands, with moist grasslands and isolated pockets of forest. There are also areas of indigenous forest along the coast.

The interior of the province consists largely of rolling hills from the Valley of A Thousand Hills to the Midlands. Many people, including one of South Africa's most well-known writers, have written about these hills. As Paton stated in his most celebrated work, *Cry, The Beloved Country*:

"There is a lovely road that runs from Ixopo into the hills. These hills are grass-covered and rolling, and they are lovely beyond any singing of it.

The road climbs seven miles into them, to Carisbrooke; and from there, if there is no mist, you look down on one of the fairest valleys of Africa.

About you there is grass and bracken and you may hear the forlorn crying of the titihoya, one of the birds of the veld. Below you is the valley of the Umzimkulu, on its journey from the Drakensberg to the sea; and beyond and behind the river, great hill after great hill; and beyond and behind them, the mountains of Ingeli and East Griqualand."

The northern part of KwaZulu-Natal Province is primarily moist savannah, whilst the Drakensberg region has mostly alpine grassland.

And while the coastal region is famous for its beaches, it also has some deep ravines and steep slopes in some parts.

KwaZulu-Natal also has many rivers. The largest is Thukela, also known as Tugela, which flows west to east across the centre of the province.

The province's subtropical climate is also characterised by a wide range of temperatures. As you move from the coast and go towards the interior, temperatures start to drop, becoming progressively colder. And some parts of the hinterland have temperatures below freezing point during winter, especially in the evening.

The Drakensberg Mountains sometimes get heavy snow in winter. And even during summer, the highest peaks occasionally get light snow.

The northern coast of the province has the warmest climate and highest humidity.

The province gets a lot of rain in summer. And it is extremely hot along the coast during summer months. The Midlands are drier than the coast and can be very cold in winter.

The KwaZulu-Natal coastline is dotted with small towns, many of which serve as seasonal recreational hubs. The coastal area's humid and subtropical climate is comparable to southern Florida's in the United States but not quite as hot and rainy in the summer.

As one moves further north up the coast towards the border with Mozambique, the climate becomes almost purely tropical. And for many people, this part of the province is a paradise for tourists. Excellent beaches, which rival the best in the world, are found along virtually every part of South Africa's eastern seaboard.

An extraordinary natural phenomenon that is witnessed annually on the KwaZulu-Natal coast during late autumn or early winter is the "sardine run."

Also referred to as "the greatest shoal on earth", the sardine run occurs when millions of sardines migrate from their spawning grounds south of the southern tip of Africa northwards along the coastline of the Eastern Cape Province towards KwaZulu-Natal following a path close to shore, often resulting in many fish washing up on beaches along the coast.

The huge shoal of tiny fish can stretch for many miles and is followed and preyed upon by thousands of predators, including game fish, sharks, dolphins and seabirds.

Usually the shoals break up and the fish disappear into deeper water around Durban. And many questions about this unusual phenomenon remain unanswered.

The biggest centre of activity on the coast is the city of Durban, the largest in KwaZulu-Natal Province.

It is also the third-largest city in South Africa and one of the fastest-growing urban areas in the world. Its harbour is the busiest in South Africa and one of the 10 largest in the world. It is also the busiest port in Africa.

Every year the port of Durban handles over 30 million tons of cargo with a value of more than R100-billion

(South African Rand - ZAR), which is equivalent to about $12.75 billion (American dollars).

To the north of Durban, is the port of Richards Bay, an important coal-export harbour which handles about 12,000 containers a year.

Combined, the two ports of Durban and Richards Bay account for about 78 per cent of South Africa's cargo tonnage.

Durban also has a very good rail network which connects it to many cities and towns throughout the entire region of Southern Africa, and not just within the country of South Africa, and is destined to play a major role in the economic growth of all the countries in the region as a major outlet to the sea and because of its excellent port facilities, the best on the entire continent.

A sprawling metropolis, Durban had a population of about 3.5 million people in 2008 but with a lower population density compared to other South African cities with the possible exception of Cape Town which also has a low population density.

The city is major tourist attraction because of its subtropical climate, excellent beaches, hotels and restaurants and other facilities.

Founded by the British in the 1830s, Durban grew through the years to become a British stronghold and remained one even during the apartheid era.

After Natal became a British colony in 1843, whites established farms, especially around Durban. But they had a problem recruiting Zulu labourers to work on their plantations.

To solve the problem, the British brought thousands of indentured labourers from India on five-year contracts. As a result of the importation of Indian labourers, Durban became a major "Asian" urban centre in South Africa and eventually had the largest Asian population in the country as it still does today.

Although Durban is located along the coast, the city

has very few flat areas. It is hilly in many areas, with some parts of the city, especially the western suburbs, being significantly higher above sea-level. Also many gorges and ravines are found within the metropolitan area. In fact, there is almost no true coastal plain in Durban despite the fact that the city is known for its excellent and modern port facilities.

Although it was founded by the British and was once mostly white, Durban today is predominantly black African and mostly Zulu.

More than 68 per cent of the city's population is black African. South Africans of Asian origin, mostly Indian, constitute the second-largest group, about 20 per cent; whites, the third-largest, about 9 per cent, and people of mixed race, or Coloureds, about 3 per cent.

The majority of the people in Durban, about 63 per cent, speak Zulu and about 30 per cent speak English. Another language spoken by a significant number of people is Xhosa. It is spoken by almost 3.5 per cent. Afrikaans is spoken by less than 2 per cent.

Other black African languages spoken in Durban include Ndebele and Sotho. Each is spoken by less than 1 per cent of the people in Durban.

The Durban metropolitan area has a large and diversified economy. Its main sectors are manufacturing, tourism, transport, and finance.

The city's coastal location and large port with excellent facilities gives it comparative advantage over many other urban and economic centres in South Africa for export-related industry.

Durban's mild climate, warm marine current and culturally diverse population have also enabled the city to become the biggest tourist destination in KwaZulu-Natal Province and one of the biggest in the entire country and in the region of Southern Africa which comprises several countries besides South Africa itself.

And remnants of British colonialism and a mix of Zulu,

Indian and Afrikaans traditions give the province a rich cultural diversity.

KwaZulu-Natal also is the only province with a monarchy specifically provided for in South Africa's Constitution.

The province also has two world heritage sites, so designated by UNESCO. Besides the Drakensberg mountain range, the other one is the Greater St Lucia Wetlands Park.

In the KwaZulu-Natal itself, the Durban metropolitan area is the biggest and most dynamic economic centre, contributing more than 50 per cent of the province's output, employment and income. The area of Durban also is the nation's second most important economic complex after Johannesburg. In fact, Durban's growth is also attributed to Johannesburg.

The port of Durban grew around trade from Johannesburg, the City of Gold, mainly because the industrial and mining capital of South Africa is landlocked and not located on any navigable body of water with direct access to the sea. Durban ended up serving that purpose as, an outlet, not only for Johannesburg but for other parts of South Africa as well.

Although much of the economy of KwaZulu-Natal revolves around Durban or the Durban metropolitan area, the province has a lot of economic potential and a fairly diversified economy.

It is mainly agricultural but with a manufacturing sector that is more developed than the other manufacturing or industrial sectors in the rest of the provinces with the exception of Gauteng and the Western Cape provinces. And the resources KwaZulu-Natal has will enable the province to achieve economic growth in the coming years if it harnesses its potential.

The province's agricultural sector is dominated by the sugar industry. In fact, sugar refining is the main industry in KwaZulu-Natal. And the main crops grown in the province include citrus fruits, maize, sorghum, beans, cotton, bananas, and pineapples.

Cattle and sheep are also raised. And dairy farming is another important part of the economy. Also a wine industry is being developed in the province.

Other industries located mainly in and around Durban include textile, motor vehicle assembly, fertiliser, rubber, paper, tannery and food processing. There are also oil refineries.

And at Richards Bay on the central coast, there are large aluminium-smelting plants. In fact, Richards Bay is the centre of operations for South Africa's aluminium industry.

Also the Richards Bay Coal Terminal has earned South Africa distinction as the second-largest exporter of steam coal in the world. And Richards Bay Minerals is the largest sand-mining and mineral-processing operation in the world.

KwaZulu-Natal Province also produces large amounts of timber.

The vehicle-manufacturing industry has created a considerable multiplier effect in component- and service-providers. The automotive leather industry has grown rapidly, with exports significantly increasing foreign exchange earnings.

KwaZulu-Natal has also recently undergone rapid industrialisation, a significant development attributed to its abundant water supply and labour resources. Industries are found at Newcastle, Ladysmith, Dundee, Richards Bay, Durban, Hammarsdale, Richmond, Pietermaritzburg and Mandeni.

Also, substantial progress has been made on the Dube Trade Port and King Shaka International Airport project at La Mercy. It is estimated that redevelopment of the current airport site will create 269,200 jobs over a 25-year period, and the airport is expected to be operational by 2010, in time for the Football World Cup.

Some of the main factors which have made agriculture central to the economy are soil fertility and abundant rain in some parts of the province, while other areas get a considerable amount of rain to support farming.

And although sugar-cane plantations along the Indian Ocean coastal belt are the mainstay of KwaZulu-Natal's agriculture, there's no question that there is an abundance of other agricultural commodities in the province. The coastal belt is also a large producer of subtropical fruit, while the farmers in the hinterland concentrate on vegetable, dairy and stock-farming.

Another major source of income is forestry, in the areas around Vryheid, Eshowe, Richmond, Harding and Ngome. Ngome also has tea plantations.

The second-largest city in KwaZulu-Natal Province is Pietermaritzburg. It is also the provincial capital. Popularly known as Maritzburg, it has a major industry producing aluminium. It also produces timber and dairy products.

Pietermaritzburg is a historic city and has the largest red-brick building of Victorian architecture in the entire southern hemisphere.

It was founded by the Boers, Voortrekkers, after they defeated the Zulu at the Battle of the Blood River and once served as the capital of Natalia, a Boer republic which lasted for only about five years from 1838 to 1843 and which later became the British colony of Natal.

After the British took over Natalia and renamed it Natal, they continued to use Pietermaritzburg as the colony's capital. After the Union of South Africa was formed in 1910, Natal became a province of the union and Pietermaritzburg remained the capital. It grew to become one of the two most important urban centres in Natal, together with Durban which was first known as Port Natal during British rule.

Pitermaritzburg was one of the most conservative cities during apartheid. But it was also in the same town where the University of Natal was founded in 1910 as the Natal University College and extended to Durban in 1922; an academic institution which played a major role in the struggle against apartheid..

The university not only played a prominent role in the struggle against apartheid; it was also one of the first universities in the country to admit black students.

The city of Pietermaritzburg occupies a special place not only in South African history but also in the history of the struggle against racial injustice beyond South Africa. It was in this town where Mahatma Gandhi launched his career which led to his becoming the apostle of non-violence emulated round the globe.

The beginning of his campaign against racial injustice is linked with an incident that took place in Pietermartizburg in which he was involved early in his life.

One day, he boarded a train in Pietermartizburg and occupied a first-class seat. But the authorities told him to get up and go to the third-class section and take a seat there. He was being asked to give up his seat in deference to a white man who had no first-class seat. Gandhi refused and was evicted from the train although he had paid for his first-class seat.

The incident inspired Gandhi to begin his career protesting against laws discriminating against Indians in South Africa. And he eventually went back to India to lead the struggle for independence by leading a campaign of non-violence against the British and won.

Among his most well-known admirers was Dr. Martin Luther King who led the civil rights movement in the United States in the sixties by using non-violent means as taught by Mahatma Gandhi.

And today, a bronze statue of Gandhi stands in the city centre of Pietermartizburg in honour of a man who influenced the world and who started his career there as an apostle of violence.

Also in 1962, Nelson Mandela was arrested in the nearby town of Howick to the north of Pietermaritzburg. The arrest marked the beginning of Nelson Mandela's 27 years of imprisonment. A small monument has been erected at the location of his arrest.

It was also in Pietermartizburg where Alan Paton, the author of *Cry, The Beloved Country* and a prominent opponent of apartheid and founder of the South African Liberal Party, was born in January 1903. He died in April 1988.

And the city continues to be remembered as one of the most historic places in the nation's history and in the history of KwaZulu-Natal Province.

Other urban centres in KwaZulu-Natal - besides Durban, Richards Bay and Pietermartizburg - also play a major role in the economy. They include towns in the interior such as Newcastle, which is well-known for steel production and coal-mining; Estcourt for meat processing, and Ladysmith and Richmond for mixed agriculture. And the KwaZulu-Natal coastal belt is well-known for its sugar cane, wood, oranges, bananas, mangoes and other tropical fruit.

Gauteng Province

GAUTENG Province is the economic powerhouse of South Africa. It has acquired this status because of Johannesburg, the City of Gold, and the mining industry probably more than anything else.

It is the smallest province in South Africa in terms of area and occupies only 1.4 per cent of the country's total area. Yet, in spite of its small size, it exercises disproportionate influence and wields enormous power over the rest of the country in vital sectors, especially financial and economic.

And it ranks second only to KwaZulu-Natal among all the provinces in terms of population. In 2008, it had a population of about 9.7 million people in an area of about 6,568 square miles.

That is a small area, and a lot of people in the province, in a country whose total area is 471,443 square miles with a population of about 44 million people. Gauteng is also the most densely populated province in the country.

Gauteng was carved out of the former Transvaal Province after the multiracial elections of 27 April 1994 which ended apartheid and was initially named Pretoria-Witwatersrand-Vereeniging (PWV). But this cumbersome name was dropped and the province was renamed Gauteng in December 1994.

Located in the heart of the Highveld in the north-eastern part of the country, Gauteng is a landlocked province. And it is the most urbanised province in South Africa and on the entire continent.

It consists of the cities of Pretoria, Johannesburg, Germiston, and Vereeniging and their surrounding metropolitan areas in the eastern part of the Witwatersrand region and is bordred by the provinces of Limpopo in the north, Mpumalanga in the east, Free State in the south, and North-West in the west.

And despite being mainly an urban province, Gauteng has a highly developed agricultural sector which is capable of providing the cities and towns with abundant food including daily fresh produce such as vegetables, fruit, meat, eggs, dairy products, as well as flowers.

In fact, Gauteng's agricultural sector is geared towards providing the cities and towns of the province with daily fresh food supplies.

Other major agricultural commodities produced in Gauteng include maize, groundnuts, sorghum, cotton and sunflowers.

A large area of the province falls within the so-called Maize Triangle. The districts of Bronkhorstspruit, Cullinan and Heidelberg have important agricultural land where ground-nuts, sunflowers, cotton and sorghum are grown.

Food, food processing and beverages make up around R9.9-billion - equivalent to about $1.25 billion (American dollars) - of the province's economy. Half of South Africa's agri-processing companies are based in Gauteng Province.

New and competitive niche products under development include organic food, essential oils, packaging, flori-culture, medicinal plants, natural remedies and health foods.

Gauteng's contribution to the national economy is huge, considering its size. It contributes 34 per cent to South Africa's economy and a phenomenal 10 per cent to the gross domestic product (GDP) of the entire African continent. It is also the continent's financial capital and with a thriving Stock Exchange.

The largest contributors to Gauteng's gross domestic product are manufacturing, finance and trade. The manufacturing sector has more than 9,300 firms and employs more than 600,00 people.

Manufacturing includes basic iron and steel, fabricated and metal products, food, machinery, electrical machinery, appliances and electrical supplies, vehicle parts and accessories, and chemical products.

Johannesburg houses the largest Stock Exchange in Africa, and Pretoria the country's Reserve Bank.

The two metropolitan areas of Johannesburg and Pretoria also have major educational and health centres which are among the best in the world.

Gauteng Province also has a highly developed infrastructure including a comprehensive road network, an international airport in Johannesburg, telecommunications facilities, and highly sophisticated financial and business institutions.

The region that came to be known as Gauteng has had a solid economic foundation since the founding of South

Africa as a nation. Even the name itself shows that very clearly. Gauteng comes from the Sotho language – Sesotho – meaning "Place of Gold."

It is the historical Sesotho name for Johannesburg and surrounding areas referring to the thriving gold industry in the province following the 1886 discovery of gold in Johannesburg.

White trekboers started entering the area from the Cape Colony after 1860. Anf after gold was discovered, it triggered a gold rush wwhich drew people from all over South Africa and other parts of the world including Britain and other parts of Europe as well as North America.

The region has 40 per cent of the world's reserves of gold and is synonymous with wealth.

But its economy has since diversified, with more sophisticated sectors such as finance and manufacturing playing a major role, and gold mining is no longer the nackbone of the province's economy.

The province is essentially one big city, with 97 per cent of its population living in urban centres. Johannesburg has the largest urban population in the province and in the entire nation.

Johannesburg is the provincial capital, and by far the biggest city in South Africa - and Africa as a whole.

Also known as Joburg, Jozi, Egoli (which means City of Gold) and by other names, it is often compared to Los Angeles, with its similar urban sprawl linked by huge highway interchanges.

And when people in other parts of Africa dream about going to South Africa, they have the City of Gold, Johannesburg, in mind probably more than any other place in that country. To many of them, it is "the land of milk and honey" on this impoverished continent.

Johannesburg is a very large city even by international standards. And it has all the facilities and social amenities of a large, highly sophisticated modern city comparable to the best in the world.

It is a single municipality that covers about 635 square miles. And it has been calculated that if a resident of the southern-most area, Orange Farm, were to walk northwards to the inner city of Johannesburg, the journey would take three days.

Mine-dumps and headgear remain symbols of Johannesburg's rich past, while modern architecture abuts fine examples of 19th-century engineering.

Gleaming skyscrapers contrast with Indian bazaars and African medicine shops, and the busy streets throng with fruit sellers and street vendors. An exciting blend of ethnic and western art and cultural activities is reflected in theatres and open-air arenas throughout the city.

South of Johannesburg is Soweto, developed as a dormitory township for black people under the apartheid system. Much of the struggle against apartheid was fought in and from Soweto, which has a population of more than two million people. Almost all of of them are black.

The urban area extends virtually uninterrupted east and west of Johannesburg through a number of towns: Roodepoort and Krugersdorp in the west, and Germiston, Springs, Boksburg and Benoni in the east.

Not only does Johannesburg have the largest economy of any metropolitan region in Africa; the city is one of the 40 largest metropolitan areas in the world. It is Africa's most developed city and one of the continent's only two global cities, the other one being Cairo.

Although Johannesburg is not one of South Africa's official national cities in terms of executive, legislative and judicial functions at the national level, it is the seat of the Constitutional Court. Bloemfotein is the nation's judicial capital, Cape Town the legislative capital, and Pretoria the administrative capital.

Located on the mineral-rich Witwatersrand range of hills, Johannesburg is the centre of the gold and diamond trade and is seen as the world's capital of the mineral industry. And it is served by O.R. Tambo International

Airport which is the largest and busiest airport in Africa and a gateway for international air travel to and from the rest of southern Africa.

The Greater Johannesburg Metropolitan Area has a population of about 8 million people, according to 2008 statistics. And the municipal city itself has about 4 million people.

The township of Soweto located southwest of Johannesburg - and whose name is an acronym derived from South West Township – is also part of Johannesburg although it is a separate administrative entity. It is a product of apartheid and was established to accommodate black migrant workers from within and outside South Africa.

About 31 miles north of Johannesburg is Pretoria, the capital of South Africa, whose southern suburbs are slowly merging with the Johannesburg sprawl. In fact, Johannesburg and Pretoria are beginning to act as one functional entity, connecting the province of Gauteng together and forming one mega-city of roughly 10 million people.

Pretoria is dominated by government services and the foreign diplomatic corps. It's also known for its colourful gardens, shrubs and trees, particularly beautiful in spring when some 50,000 jacaranda trees envelop the avenues in mauve. It is also known as the Jacaranda City and had a population of about one million people in 2008.

Also, Pretoria's main street, Church Street, is said to be the longest urban street in South Africa and one of the longest straight streets in the world.

The Pedi, with a population of about 440,000, constitute the largest ethnic group in Pretoria followed by Afrikaners, with about 423,000, and then the Tswana with about 340,000 people.

Others are Zulu, about 151,000; whites of British descent, Ndebele, Sotho, Swati, Xhosa, and Venda. There are other groups as well, including immigrants.

Pretoria was founded in 1855 by Voortrekkers. It was named after Andries Pretorius who became a hero of the Voortrekkers after his victory over the Zulu in the Battle of the Blood River, one of the bloodiest and most important events in the history of South Africa. It was once the capital of Transvaal and when South Africa became a republic in 1961, Pretoria remained its administrative capital, hence the capital of the apartheid regime.

Because of the nature of the regime, Pretoria also became a monument to white supremacy.

And the name still has a negative connotation among many black South Africans. A significant number of them want to change the name of the city and rename it Tshwane after an African chief who once ruled the area. But the proposed change has triggered stiff opposition from the white community, especially Afrikaners who see it as an assault on their heritage. And it remains a highly controversial subject among the majority of the city's residents.

The province of Gauteng also has important industrial and coal-mining towns, Vereeniging and Vanderbiljpark, in the southern part on the Vaal River.

Slightly smaller than the American state of New Jersey, Gauteng Province has vast contrasts in its climate. It gets rain in the summer. But the province has hot summers and cold winters with frost. And hail is common during summer thunderstorms.

Life in Gauteng also provides sharp contrasts. It has some of the richest people in South Africa and in the entire the world, also some of the poorest. The people of Gauteng also have the highest per capita in the entire country.

The province blends cultures, colours, and First and Third-World traditions in a spirited mix, flavoured by a number of foreign influences. The world's languages can be heard on the streets and in offices, from English to Mandarin, Swahili, French, German and much more.

It is rich cultural mix of stunning diversity in the African context somewhat reminiscent of New York City which has attracted people from all countries and cultures round the globe without parallel in world history.

That is what prompts many Africans in other parts of the continent to say, gleefully, "South Africa is our New York," even when they are not always welcome there. And the largest number of them flock to Johannesburg.

Gauteng also has the most important educational and health centres in the country.

Johannesburg has the University of the Witwatersrand, often simply known as Wits, which is regarded by many people to be the foremost academic institution in the country and of international stature; while Pretoria boasts the largest residential university in South Africa, the University of Pretoria, and what is believed to be the largest correspondence university in the world, the University of South Africa which is also often simply known by its initials, UNISA.

The South African Council for Scientific and Industrial Research (CSIR) is also located in Pretoria.

Pretoria is also a major industrial centre with heavy industries such as iron and steel casting as well as motor vehicle, railway and machinery manufacturing.

And according to a study entitled *An Inquiry into Cities and Their Role in Subnational Economic Growth in South Africa* by some economists at Potchefstroom University published in 2002, Pretoria contributes 8.55 per cent of the country's total gross domestic product (GDP) making it the third-biggest contributor after Johannesburg and Cape Town.

The significance of Gauteng Province can also be looked at from another perspective. More than 60 per cent of South Africa's research and development (R&D) takes place in Gauteng, which has 41 per cent of the country's core biotechnology companies.

It's also home to leading research institutions such as

the Council for Scientific and Industrial Research CSIR), the Agricultural Research Council and the Onderstepoort Veterinary Institute.

And although the province is highly urbanised and industrialised, it contains wetlands of international importance, such as Blesbokspruit near Springs.

Gauteng also is home to one of South Africa's seven UNESCO World Heritage sites. The region of Sterkfontein, Swartkrans, Kromdraai – and surrounding areas – has one of the world's richest concentrations of hominid fossils.

The most important economic sectors are financial and business services, logistics and communications, and mining.

Gauteng, especially Johannesburg, is not only the financial capital of Africa; more than 70 foreign banks have their head offices in the province, and at least just as many South African banks, stockbrokers and insurance giants. The JSE in Johannesburg is the 17th largest stock exchange in the world by market capitalisation.

As the leading economic region in South Africa in terms of wealth, Gauteng also has taken the lead in the country in terms of diversification.

The province's economy is moving away from traditional heavy industry markets and low value-added production towards sophisticated high value-added production, particularly in information technology, telecoms and other high-tech industries.

In an international survey in 2000, Gauteng was identified as one of 46 global hubs of technological innovation. The burgeoning high-tech corridor in Midrand, halfway between Pretoria and Johannesburg, is the fastest-developing area in the country.

The province has the best telecommunications and technology on the continent, with correspondents for the world's major media stationed there, as well as South Africa's five television stations. It also has the highest concentration of radio, internet and print media in the whole of Africa.

Besides its sophisticated infrastructure, the province is also well-endowed by nature. In addition to its minerals, Gauteng also has an excellent climate which has enabled it to grow a variety of crops in abundance. It also has a beautiful landscape.

Most of Gauteng is on the Highveld, a high-altitude grassland. Between Johannesburg and Pretoria there are low parallel ridges and undulating hills, some part of the Magaliesberg Mountains and the Witwatersrand. The north of the province is more subtropical due to its lower altitude and is mostly dry savannah.

Even though the province is at a subtropical altitude, the climate is comparatively cooler especially in the Johannesburg area. And humidity is not a major problem. Winters are crisp and dry with frost occurring often in the southern areas. Snow is very rare, but has occurred on some occasions in the Johannesburg metropolitan area.

The province's demographic profile also makes Gauteng stand out among all the provinces in South Africa. With almost 20 per cent of the nation's total population, Gauteng is also the fastest-growing province in the country.

The province also has an ethnic diversity within the African population and a racial composition which reflect balance not found anywhere else in South Africa. There is no single black African ethnic group whose people vastly outnumber others as, for example, the Zulu do in KwaZulu-Natal and the Xhosa in the Eastern Cape Province.

About 21 per cent of the people in Gauteng Province speak Zulu; 14.4 per cent speak Afrikaans, 13.1 per cent speak Sotho, and 12.5 per cent speak English. Many black Africans speak English and Afrikaans and are included in these statistics.

The vast majority of the people are black African. They

constitute a formidable 73.8 per cent but are divided along ethnic lines in terms of identity and affiliation, although many of them also collectively identify themselves as black Africans. Some may even simply as South Africans transcending racial and ethnic identities, although this is rare just as it is among the people of other races.

And although blacks constitute about 74 per cent of Gauteng's population, whites also make a significant number, about 20 per cent, of the entire population in the province. Coloureds constitute about 4 per cent, and Asians, mostly Indian, about 2.5 per cent.

Among black Africans, there are other black African languages which are spoken by a significant number of people besides Zulu and Sotho which have the largest number of speakers more than any other African languages but not in overwhelming numbers.

Other black African languages spoken in Gauteng Province include Ndebele which is spoken by about 2 per cent of the people; Xhosa spoken by about 7.6 per cent; Sepedi, 10.7 per cent; Tswana, 8.4 per cent; Swati, 1.4 per cent; Venda, 1.7 per cent; Tsonga, by about 5.7 per cent. And about 1 per cent of the people – of all races – speak a non-official language at home.

The term "official language" in this context refers to the 11 official languages of South Africa. They include English and Afrikaans, and nine other languages spoken by nine of South Africa's indigenous groups: IsiNdebele, IsiXhosa, Isi Zulu, Sepedi, Sesotho, Setswana, SiSwati, Tshivenda, and Xitsonga.

South Africa also recognises eight non-official languages: Fanagalo, Lobedu, Northern Ndebele, Phuthi, Khoi, Nama, and San. They are all typical black African languages except Fanagalo which is a pidgin - a hybrid - derived from a combination of Zulu, English and Afrikaans. But it is essentially Zulu.

All these languages are also spoken in Gauteng Province just as they are in other parts of South Africa.

Gauteng is not only the economic hub of South Africa which contributes heavily in the financial, manufacturing, transport, technology and telecommunications sectors among others; it is also hosts - more than any other country on the continent - a large number of overseas companies requiring a commercial base in and gateway to Africa.

Rapid economic and population growth is also anticipated for Gauteng Province. It is growing rapidly due to mass urbanisation that is a feature of many developing countries. According to the State of the Cities Report, the urban portion of Gauteng - comprised primarily of the cities of Johannesburg, Ekurhuleni (the East Rand) and Tshwane (greater Pretoria) - will be a polycentric urban region with a projected population of some 14.6 million people by 2015, making it one of the largest cities in the world.

But the AIDS epidemic may have a devastating impact on that, reducing the number significantly, unless something is done to control the disease.

The rapid growth of Gauteng has brought with it both opportunities and challenges.

As a global focal point, with access to the Southern African hinterland, Gauteng has the ability to link the world to a population approximately the same size as the United States. It is fast becoming to sub-Saharan Africa what the Eastern Seaboard megalopolis is to the United States.

But this also presents some formidable obstacles, most notably the ability to provide access to basic amenities such as electricity and potable water.

Transport also is a major problem, and Johannesburg, as the hub of Gauteng, is beginning to experience the heavy traffic problems of cities such as Los Angeles and Bangkok. There are plans to improve transport which include the construction of a high-speed railway between Pretoria, Sandton, Johannesburg and Oliver Tambo

International Airport. The railway is expected to be completed in 2010.

But whatever the problems the provinces faces, its prospects for further development are bright because of its abundant resources, highly developed infrastructure, and excellent schools.

It is probably the leading centre of learning in South Africa and has many universities and other academic institutions It is also the centre of South Africa's research and development (R&D) with the best facilities on the entire continent.

Limpopo Province

LIMPOPO is the fifth-largest province in South Africa in terms of area, and the fourth-largest in terms of population.

It is slightly larger than the American state of Pennsylvania and has an area of 47,838 square miles which is about 10.3 per cent of the entire area of South Africa. And the province had a population of more than 5.4 million people in 2008.

It is also South Africa's northernmost province, lying within the great curve of the Limpopo River. The river is one of the largest in Africa and it flows along South Africa's northern border with Botswana and Zimbabwe.

It is also known as the Crocodile River, and many African immigrants trying to cross the river on their way to South Africa have drowned in this river or have been eaten by crocodiles through the years. And it is navigable for only about 130 miles.

Limpopo Province includes the former homelands – or Bantustans – of Gazankulu and Venda and parts of Lebowa.

The province is a land of remarkable contrasts, ranging

from true bushveld country to majestic mountains, primeval indigenous forests, unspoilt wilderness and patchworks of farmland.

The province borders the countries of Botswana in the west and northwest, Zimbabwe in the north and northeast, and by Mozambique in the east.

In the eastern region of the province lies the northern half of the magnificent Kruger National Park, a nature reserve teeming with African wildlife in a total area roughly the size of Israel.

But, despite its attraction as a haven for wildlife, this region has also proved to be deadly in many cases. Through the years, a number of African immigrants from Mozambique and other parts of Africa have been killed by lions and other animals in this area of Kruger National Park in their desperate attempt to sneak into South Africa in search of jobs and better life.

Yet the national park is one of the greatest treasures the province – indeed the entire nation – has.

The northern section of the Kruger National Park, which is located in Limpopo, is renowned for its large herds of elephant and buffalo, significant numbers of tsessebe and sable and a rich bird life.

On the western border of the park, there are excellent privately-owned game reserves and lodges which provide game viewing day and night. And the mountainous area of Waterberg in the northern part of the province is also home to numerous game reserves.

The Waterberg region also has magnificent baobab trees. They're found throughout the area.

The Soutpansberg range is one of the most spectacular regions of South Africa. Beyond the mountains, mopane trees and giant, ancient baobab trees dominate the plains sweeping northward to Zimbabwe. Many natural heritage sites in the area are accessible to visitors. And there are 340 indigenous tree species here, an abundance of animal life and the world's highest concentration of leopard.

It may not be paradise on earth in the wilderness in this part of South Africa in Limpopo Province but it's pretty close to that.

The area of what came to be known as Limpopo Province was once a part the Transvaal and was initially named Northern Transvaal when the country was re-organised in 1994 after the end of apartheid, creating new provinces. But in 1995, it was renamed Northern Province. Then in June 2003, its name was changed again and the province came be known as Limpopo. It was named after its famous river.

It was also almost named Mapungubwe, after an area where the oldest community in the province which used gold for centuries was discovered. The Mapungubwe cultural landscape is on the southern banks of the Limpopo River. Archaeologists believe that the iron-age sites of Mapungubwe were once the capitals of ancient African kings or rulers.

The vast majority of the people in Limpopo Province are black African. They constitute a formidable 97.3 per cent of the total population. Whites make up 2.4 per cent, Coloureds 0.2 per cent, and Asians, mostly of Indian origin, 0.1 per cent.

The most widely spoken languages in the province are Sesotho (Northern Sotho also known as Sepedi), Xitsonga, Tshivenda and Afrikaans.

Sepedi or Northern Sotho is the most widely spoken language. It is spoken by 57 per cent of the people in Limpopo Province; Tsonga by 23 per cent, Venda by 12 per cent, and Afrikaans by 2.6 per cent.

Those figures also reflect the demographic composition of the province, with the Sepedi (or Northern Sotho) constituting the majority of the people in Limpopo, followed by the Tsonga. English-speaking whites are less than half a per cent of the province's total population.

Limpopo Province occupies what is probably the most strategic location among all the South African provinces in terms of direct contact with other African countries because it shares borders with three of them. It therefore provides a link between South Africa and the countries to the north.

And on its southern flank from east to west, the province shares regional borders with the provinces of Mpumalanga, Gauteng, and the North West.

Its border with Gauteng includes that province's Johannesburg-Pretoria axis, the most industrialised metropole on the continent. Thus the province is placed at the centre of regional, national, and international developing markets.

The province has excellent road, rail, and air links. The N1 route from Johannesburg, which extends the length of the province, is the busiest overland route in Africa in terms of cross-border trade in raw materials and beneficiated goods.

The port of Durban in KwaZulu-Natal Province, Africa's busiest, is served directly by the province, as are the ports of Richards Bay, also in KwaZulu-Natal, and Maputo which is also the capital of the neighbouring country of Mozambique. And the Gateway International Airport is situated in Polokwane, the capital of the province.

Polokwane was once called Pietersburg, and many people still call it that. The provincial government changed the town's name to Polokwane in June 2003. Polokwane means "place of safety."

It became a city in April 1992 and is now the major urban centre – in addition to being the provincial capital - not only in Limpopo Province but for the entire area of South Africa north of Gauteng Province.

And it was in Polokwane where the country's ruling African National Congress held its national conference in December 2007 and elected Jacob Zuma to be the leader of the party, virtually anointing to be the next president of South Africa in 2009.

The town was founded by the Boers – Voortrekkers – in 1886 and named it Pietersburg in honour of Petrus Jacobus Joubert, a Voortrekker leader.

Located in the middle of the province, Polokwane had a population of more than 300,000 in 2008, mostly black African. And about 10 per cent of the entire population of Limpopo Province lives in the municipal area of Polokwane.

The municipality of Polokwane includes rural areas surrounding the city, and most of the people in the municipality live in rural areas; with the urban area constituting the inner core surrounded by rural villages which constitute the largest segment of the municipal area. And because it is the province's economic centre, Polokwane has a high population density compared to other parts of Limpopo Province.

Polokwane also is a major commercial and agricultural centre, as well as a cultural hub of the region featuring many art exhibitions and historical buildings. And in spite of its rural setting and surroundings, it is a relatively modern city with wide streets, jacaranda and coral trees, colourful parks and sparkling fountains.

Also around Polokwane are some of the best cattle ranches in the entire South Africa.

And because of its strategic location bordering three countries, the province of Limpopo has a lot of potential to develop economically.

One of the inter-territorial projects is the Maputo Development Corridor linking the province directly with the Port of Maputo in Mozambique, creating development and trade opportunities, particularly in the southeastern part of the province.

Limpopo Province connects to the corridor via the Phalaborwa Spatial Development Initiative, a network of rail and road corridors linked to major seaports. This is complemented by airports in centres such as Phalaborwa and Musina, as well as the Gateway International Airport in Polokwane.

In the northern part of the province is Modimolle, the hub of the local table-grape industry set near the beautiful Waterberg mountain range; Makhado at the foot of the Soutpansberg mountains; and Musina, with its thick-set baobab trees.

Other important Limpopo towns include the major mining centres of Phalaborwa and Thabazimbi, and Tzaneen, a producer of tea, forestry products and tropical fruit. Bela-Bela, with its popular mineral water baths, is near the southern border.

Through the centre of the province runs the Great North Road, an important route into Africa, which crosses into Zimbabwe at the major border post of Beit Bridge, all the way to Zambia, Tanzania, Kenya and up to Cairo in Egypt. The Great North Road is also simply known as C to C: Cape to Cairo.

Limpopo Province is in the savannah, an area of mixed grassland and trees generally known as bushveld. A summer-rainfall region, the northern and eastern areas are subtropical with hot and humid summers and mist in the mountains. Winter is mild and mostly frost-free.

The province is rich in natural beauty, culture and widlife, and has a thriving tourism industry. In addition to the Kruger National Park, there are 54 provincial reserves and several luxury private game reserves in Limpopo.

It's also home to the Mapungubwe Cultural Landscape, one of the country's seven World Heritage sites.

South Africa's first kingdom, Mapungubwe developed into the subcontinent's largest realm, lasting for 400 years before it was abandoned in the 14th century. Its highly sophisticated people traded gold and ivory with China, India and Egypt.

Valuable archaeological artefacts have been discovered in the area, which lies on the open savannah of the Mapungubwe National Park at the confluence of the Limpopo and Shashe Rivers.

Also known as the Great North, the province of Limpopo is rich in history. There are ruins and relics which have existed in the forests for centuries. They include the Stone Age and Iron Age relics of Makapansgat Valley and the reasures of Mapungubwe.

The first wave of black African immigrants from East and Central Africa crossed the great Limpopo River and settled in the region while others moved farther south before 300 A.D. So, even back then, what is Limpopo Province today was the gateway to South Africa.

It was also the scene of conflict and witnessed some of the bitterest conflicts in South African history. When the Voortrekkers arrived in Limpopo in the early 19th century, numerous battles between the indigenous people and the new settlers were fought on this land.

The province is rich in history. And much has not changed for centuries. In many parts of the province, you see Africa in its pristine beauty. It is also a place of legend. This is the home of Modjadji, the fabled and enigmatic Rain Queen who is said to have the mystical power to make rain.

But that's not all. There's a lot more in this province in the northern part of South Africa.

At many archaeological sites, a lot from the past is still being discovered, sometimes with amazing frequency to baffle even some of the most optimistic souls, in spite of the painstaking work. The more they discover, the more they realise how little they know about the place. It goes on and on, though it's an experience not unique to Limpopo Province.

In the Makapans Caves near Mokopane are some of the oldest evident remains of prehistoric human habitation. Other parts of the province have equally interesting prehistoric and archaeological sites.

The province is also rich in minerals. Mineral deposits found in Limpopo Province include platinum group metals, iron ore, chromium high- and middle-grade coking coal, diamonds, antimony, phosphate and copper, as well as mineral reserves like gold, emeralds, scheelite, magnetite, vermiculite, silicon and mica.

Base commodities such as black granite, corundum and feldspar are also found. And mining contributes more than a fifth of the province's economic output.

Limpopo Province is a typical developing area, exporting primary products and importing manufactured goods and services. It has a high potential for development, with resources such as tourism, rain-fed agriculture, minerals and abundant labour offering excellent investment opportunities.

The province is also well-known for its agriculture. The bushveld is cattle country, where extensive ranching operations are often supplemented by controlled hunting. About 80 per cent of South Africa's hunting industry is in Limpopo.

Sunflowers, cotton, maize and groundnuts are cultivated in the Bela-Bela and Modimolle areas. Modimolle is also known for its table-grape crops.

Tropical fruit such as bananas, litchis, pineapples, mangoes and pawpaws, as well as a variety of nuts, are grown in the Tzaneen and Makhado areas. Tzaneen is also at the centre of extensive tea and coffee plantations.

And More than 45 per cent of the R2-billion (about $252 million – US Dollars) annual turnover of the Johannesburg Fresh Produce Market comes from Limpopo.

The province also produces about 75 per cent of South Africa's mangoes, 65 per cent of its papayas, 36 per cent of its tea, 25 per cent of its citrus, bananas, and litchis, 60 per cent of its avocados, 60 per cent of its tomatoes, 35 per cent of its oranges, and 285,000 tons of potatoes.

And the largest tomato farm in South Africa is in Limpopo Province. It is located between between Tzaneen and Makhado.

Extensive forestry plantations are also found in the

region, including hardwood which is in very high demand in furniture manufacturing.

In addition to commercial agriculture for which Limpopo is renowned throughout the country and beyond, subsistence farming is the backbone of the economy for the majority of the people in the rural areas throughout the province.

Primarily agricultural, rich in spectacular scenery and a wealth of historical and cultural treasures, Limpopo Province is in many fundamental respects typical of the rest of sub-Saharan Africa. But it is also different from the countries and regions beyond South Africa precisely for that reason. It is an integral part of South Africa, not the rest of Africa.

Limpopo is the last province people see when they leave South Africa headed north. It is also the first province people see when they enter South Africa from the north. And it is, in some ways, a bridge between two worlds: the "first world" of relatively affluent South Africa and the "third world" of the rest of sub-Saharan Africa.

Mpumalanga Province

MPUMALANGA Province is in the northeastern part of South Africa north of KwaZulu-Natal Province.

The name Mpumalanga comes from the Swazi language and it means "a place where the sun rises."

It became a province, as did the rest, on 27 April 1994 after the old provinces were abolished when apartheid ended.

During the apartheid era, it was part of Transvaal Province. After it was carved out of that province, it was first named Eastern Transvaal until its named was changed to Mpumalanga in August 1995.

It is the eighth-largest province, out of nine provinces,

and has an area of 30,691 square miles which constitutes 6.5 per cent of South Africa's land area. In 2008, it had more than 3.5 million people and ranked fifth among all the provinces in terms of population.

The vast majority of the people are black Africa. They constitute 92.4 per cent of the population in Mpumalanga Province. Whites make up 6.5 per cent, Coloureds 0.2 per cent, and Asians, mostly of Indian origin, 0.2 per cent.

The largest black African ethnic group is the Swati, and 30.8 per cent of the people in the entire province speak SiSwati, while 26.4 per cent speak IsiZulu, 12.1 per cent IsiNdebele, and 10.8 per cent speak Sepedi (Northern Sotho).

Mpumalanga is bordered by Limpopo Province in the north; by Mozambique in the east and northeast; Swaziland in the east and southeast; KwaZulu-Natal in the south, the Free State in the southwest, and by Gauteng in the west.

It includes the former homelands or Bantustans of KwaNdebele, KaNgwane, and parts of Lebowa and Bophuthatswana.

Endowed with magnificent scenic beauty and abundance of wildlife, it is a have for tourists. The province lies on the high plateau grasslands of the Middleveld which roll eastwards for hundreds of miles of virtually unspoiled land.

And in the northeast, it rises towards mountain peaks and terminates in an immense escarpment. In places this escarpment plunges hundreds of metres down to the low-lying area known as the Lowveld.

In the eastern region lies the southern half of the magnificent Kruger National Park, a nature reserve teeming with African wildlife in a total area roughly the size of Israel.

The Drakensberg escarpment divides Mpumalanga into halves: the western part of high-altitude grassland (the Highveld) and the eastern region which lies at a low altitude in the subtropical Lowveld/Bushveld that is mostly savannah. And the southern half of Kruger National Park is located in this eastern part of Mpumalanga bordering Mozambique, while the northern half of the park is in Limpopo Province.

The central part of Mpumalanga, dominated by the Drakensberg, is very mountainous because of this range of mountains which in most places in this province exceed 6562 feet.

The Lowveld is relatively flat with interspersed rocky outcrops. And the Lebombo Mountains which are in the far eastern part of the province form a low range and lie along the border with Mozambique.

Mpumalanga has another range of mountains, the Crocodile River Mountains, which are in the sosutheastern part of the province.

There are also remarkable contrasts in the climate of the province. Because of its proximity to the Indian Ocean and lower altitude, the region that is known as the Lowveld is subtropical, while the Highveld is comparatively much cooler at an altitude of 5580 feet to 7546 feet.

The Drakensberg escarpment gets the highest amount of precipitation, because of its very high altitude, while all the other areas of the province get a considerable amount of rain which falls in summer accompanied by thunderstorms.

The Highveld experiences severe frost a lot of times contrasted with the Lowveld which is mostly frost-free.

There is very little rainfall in winter except for some drizzle on the Drakensberg escarpment.

A large area of Mpumalanga Province is an integral part of an animal park which transcends national boundaries: the Great Limpopo Transfrontier Park, once known Gaza-Kruger-Gonarezhou Transfrontier Park.

This international game park brings together some of the best and most established wildlife areas in southern

Africa. It is managed as an integrated unit across three national borders. The mega-park includes the Kruger National Park in South Africa, the Limpopo National Park in Mozambique, and the Gonarezhou National Park in Zimbabwe.

And there are many other game sanctuaries in Mpumalanga Province. They include private game reserves.

As in most parts of South Africa, climate plays a major role in the economic well-being of the people in Mpumalanga Province and in the economic prosperity of the province as a whole. Major contrasts in climate between the drier Highveld region with its cold winters and the hot, humid Lowveld have enabled the people of Mpumalanga to engage in a variety of agricultural activities at the subsistence and commercial levels.

Almost 70 per cent of the land in Mpumalanga is used for agriculture. Crops include maize, wheat, sorghum, barley, sunflower seeds, soybeans, groundnuts, sugar cane, vegetables, coffee, tea, cotton, tobacco, as well as citrus, subtropical and deciduous fruit.

It's a wide range of agricultural commodities for local consumption and export. The province's agricultural commodities are used at the subsistence level and for commercial purposes within and outside the province.

Forestry also is an integral part of the economy, especially in the northern part of the province. The province also one of South Africa's largest paper mills located at Ngodwana. And the areas of Sabie and Graskop provide a large part of the country's total requirement for forestry products.

These forestry plantations are also an ideal backdrop for ecotourism opportunities, with a variety of popular hiking trails, a myriad waterfalls, patches of indigenous forest and many nature reserves.

Mpumalanga Province also has the largest natural freshwater lake in South Africa, Lake Chrissie, which is famous for its variety of aquatic birds, particularly flamingos.

A lot of land in the province is also used for grazing. The area used for grazing constitutes 14 per cent of the province's land area and plays a major role in the production of beef, mutton, wool, poultry and dairy products.

One of the most important sectors of the economy is mining. Extensive mining is done in Mpumalanga and the province has a wide range of minerals. They include platimum group of metals, gold, chromite, silica, cobalt, zinc, antimony, manganese, copper, iron, tin, coal, asbestos, limestone, talc, magnesite, shale, and others.

In fact, Mpumalanga Province produces 83 per cent of South Africa's entire coal output. And that is critical because 90 per cent of the nation's coal is used to produce electricity and synthetic fuel. So the province plays a very important role in the nation's well-being. South Africa is one of the leading countries in the world in the production of petrol and other fuels from coal.

Mpumalanga is home to South Africa's major coal-fired power stations three of which are the biggest in the southern hemisphere. Witbank is the biggest coal producer in Africa, while Its is the site of the country's second oil-from-coal plant after Sasolburg.

And with an entire half of Kruger National Park on its territory, Mpumalanga Province is one of the biggest tourist destinations in South Africa and on the entire continent. The entire park in Mpumalanga and Limpopo provinces covers an area of 7,800 square miles and is one of the most well-known parks in the world.

Other major tourist attractions in Mpumalanga Province include the ancient Sudwala Caves. They are said to be the oldest caves in the world. And they were formed naturally. They were once used by the Swazi as a place of refuge; and they were later used by the Boers to store ammunition.

The major chamber in the Sudwala Caves has been used as a concert hall on a number of occasions. The other chambers include some with calcium structures. And some are crystal chambers.

The largest city in the province is Nelspruit. It also serves as the provincial capital.

Located on the Crocodile River in the Lowveld, Nelspruit is about 60 miles west of the border with Mozambique and 205 miles east of Johannesburg. It is also the administrative and business hub of the Lowveld.

It was founded in 1905 and is a major manufacturing and agricultural centre for northeastern South Africa. Major industries include citrus fruit canning, paper production, furniture manufacturing, and timber production..

Also fertile soils and a subtropical climate are an ideal combination for the growing citrus and tropical fruits. Fruits grown include mangoes, bananas, avocados and Macadamia nuts.

Other crops grown in Mpumalanga include nuts, pawpaws, granadillas, guavas, litchis, and a variety of vegetables.

Groblersdal is an important irrigation area, yielding crops such as citrus, cotton, tobacco, wheat and vegetables. And Carolina-Bethal-Ermelo is mainly a sheep-farming area but potatoes, sunflowers, maize and groundnuts are also produced in the region.

There are also many orange farms in the area around Nelspruit. In fact, Nelspruit is the second-largest citrus-producing area in South Africa and is the source of one third of the country's export in oranges.

The city also is home to the Government Research Institute for Citrus and Subtropical Fruits and the Lowveld Botanical Gardens.

Nelspruit also is a major transit point for tourists travelling to Kruger National Park and to neighbouring Mozambique. And tourists from Mozambique also play a major role in the city's economy primarily as consumers spending a lot of money when they are in town.

During the Boer War, Nelspruit briefly served as the capital of the Boer Republic.

Although Mpumalanga Province is primarily rural and is one of the least urbanised provinces in South Africa, it has other important towns, besides Nelspruit, which serve as business and tourist centres. But they are basically small.

The provincial economy also has several important sectors in different parts of the province which include urban centres.

Witbank is the centre of the local coal-mining industry; Standerton in the south is known for its large dairy industry; and Piet Retief in the southeast is a production area for tropical fruit and sugar.

A large sugar industry is also found at Malelane in the east. Ermelo is the district in South Africa that produces the most wool; Barberton is one of the oldest gold-mining towns in South Africa; and Sabie is situated in the forestry heartland of the country.

The Maputo Development Corridor, which links Mpumalanga Province with Gauteng Province and the port of Maputo in Mozambique, heralds a new era of economic development and growth for the region. As the first international toll road in Africa, the corridor is going to attract investment and help harness the economic potential of Mpumalanga and other landlocked parts of the country.

Mpumalanga also stands out among all the South African provinces in another fundamental respect. It is the largest production region for forestry and agriculture in the entire country.

Mining, manufacturing and electricity contribute to 41.4 per cent of the province's gross domestic product (GDP), with the remainder coming from government services, agriculture, forestry and related industries.

Mpumalanga is the fourth-biggest contributor to the country's gross domestic product.

Other important products from Mpumalanga are steel and vanadium which are produced in Middleburg.

The best-performing sectors in the province include mining, manufacturing and services. And tourism as well as agri-processing have a lot of potential which could lead to the growth and expansion of these sectors on a large scale in a relatively few years.

And just as Limpopo Province serves a bridge, and as a conduit, between South Africa and the countries to the north, Mpumalanga also serves as a bridge and as a conduit between South Africa and the countries of Mozambique and Swaziland and beyond. in the eastern part of the continent.

And both provide the first window into South Africa for those travelling on land on their way to the most developed country on the continent.

Part III:

The People

ALTHOUGH South Africa is one of the largest countries in Africa in terms of area and population, it has one of the smallest numbers of ethnic groups – or tribes – on the entire continent.

To illustrate the point, here are two examples: The Democratic Republic of Congo (DRC), a country of comparable size in terms of population, has about 200 ethnic groups; and Tanzania, which is bigger than Nigeria in terms of area but with only about a third of Nigeria's population – roughly 40 million – has about 130 ethnic groups.

By remarkable contrast, South Africa has fewer than 20. Yet it has the biggest population among all the countries of Southern Africa.

We are going to take a look at some of South Africa's ethnic groups to get a better understanding of this vibrant nation which is also, in many ways, the beacon of Africa and one of the most influential countries in the entire Third World.

South Africa has about 45 million people. About 31 million of them are black African, 5 million white, 3 million Coloured, and I million of Asian origin, mostly Indian.

South Africa's population also is one of the most complex and diverse in the entire world. And on the African continent, South Africa has the largest number of whites, people of mixed race, and those of Asian origin. No other country on the continent comes even close to that.

The black African population is divided into four major ethnic groups, quite often with overlapping identities in terms of culture among the major groups and others within each of those groups mainly because of their common origin and shared history.

The four main groups are the Nguni, the Sotho, the Shangaan-Tsonga, and the Venda.

There are many subgroups. The Zulu are the largest, and the Xhosa the second-largest. Both belong to the Nguni main group.

Among whites, Afrikaans constitute the largest group. They make up 60 per cent of the white population. The remaining 40 per cent are mainly of British descent, although there are other people of European origin who are included in this percentage but on a much smaller scale.

People of mixed race, collectively known as Coloureds, live mostly in the Northern Cape and Western cape Provinces. And most of the Indians live in KwaZulu-Natal. Afrikaners are concentrated in Gauteng and Free State, and most whites of British descent live in the Western Cape, Eastern Cape and KwaZulu-Natal provinces.

There are eleven official languages, as we learnt earlier: English, Afrikaans, Zulu, Xhosa, Tsonga, Tswana, Ndebele, Swazi, Venda, Sepedi, and Southern Sotho. They are different, yet many of them are related.

The people who belong to the Bantu linguistic family

in South Africa migrated from the area of East and Central Africa which includes the Great Lakes region.

The Bantu people who migrated to South Africa from this region are collectively known as Nguni. And they are divided into two major groups: the Northern Nguni, and the Southern Nguni.

The Northern Nguni include the Zulu; the Swazi; and the Shangaan who are found on both sides of the South African-Mozambican border.

The Southern Nguni include the Xhosa who constitute the largest group in this Southern Nguni family. Other Southern Nguni groups include the Thembu and the Mpondo who are also subgroups of the Xhosa.

And four of South Africa's 11 official language are Nguni languages: isiZulu, isXhosa, isiNdebele, and siSwati. Each of these languages has regional variants and dialects which are often mutually intelligible.

The Nguni social structure was also different from that of other groups such as the Northern Sotho whose homesteads were consolidated into villages. Before the 19th century, the Nguni did not have that. They had dispersed households, not villages.

And cattle were a very important part of their economy and social life. They also grew crops and did some hunting.

Their system of government revolved around small chiefdoms which were not united before the 18th century. But the people were also free to leave and join another chiefdom or form their own if they were not satisfied with th leadership.

There were some larger chiefdoms which sometimes controlled smaller ones, but such control was limited and did not last for more than a generation or two. Probably the main reason they did not last long is that the people resented too much control and hated dictatorship, in spite of their great loyalty to a ruler who was good to them.

One of the most prominent Nguni groups that evolved

through the years were the Zulu who still exist today as a powerful ethnic entity.

The Zulu, whose correct name is amaZulu according to themselves, believe that they are descended from a leader named Zulu who was born a Nguni chief in the Congo Basin area centuries ago.

In the 16th century, they migrated south and eventually settled in the eastern part of South Africa, an area now known as KwaZulu-Natal.

When they arrived in South Africa, they came into contact with the San and adopted many of their customs. They also borrowed some words from the San and other linguistic features.

During the reign of Shaka, who was the leader of the Zulu nation from 1816 to 1828, the Zulu were the most powerful kingdom in South Africa and a formidable military force.

And they have remained an influential force in South African life throughout the nation's history.

The basic unit of Zulu society was *imizi*, a homestead consisting of an extended family. Obligations to the well-being of this social unit were determined by gender. Men were responsible for defending the family members, building homes, taking care of cattle, making farm implements as well as weapons. And women were responsible for growing and taking care of crops on land near the family compounds.

Zulu chiefs collected large amounts of tribute and taxes from their subjects and in many cases they became very wealthy. They also commanded large armies and invaded weaker chiefdoms, annexing them. Men who distinguished themselves in war enhanced their status and became leaders. Shaka, who was a warrior, is a typical example. He became a leader and built the Zulu empire. He began building the empire in 1817 but after his death less than 10 years later in 1828, the Zulu empire disintegrated.

However, the Zulu survived as a single ethnic entity,

even if not under one leadership, and their common culture played a major role in holding the people together, as did their common history including pride in the Zulu empire that once reigned supreme over a vast expanse of territory in southern Africa. This ethnic consciousness among the Zulu is still very strong even today.

The Zulu are known throughout the world as formidable fighters, clearly demonstrated by their prowess in the wars against the British during the conquest of South Africa in the 19th century during which they inflicted heavy casualties on the imperial forces, although they were eventually defeated.

They are also well-known for their bead-work and basketry as well as music.

They are mostly farmers and raise cattle. One of the most important crops they grow is maize, an integral part of their diet together with vegetables and meat.

The men and the boys take care of the cows, and till the land, while women do most of the planting and harvesting in addition to the responsibilities they have at home raising children and taking care of the household.

Although many Zulus are Christians, there are those who still adhere to their traditional religion. And even among some of those who practice Christianity, traditional religious beliefs still play a role in their lives, in varying degrees depending on individual and family interests.

Zulu traditional religion is based on the existence of a Supreme Being called Nkulunkulu. The Zulu also believe that the dead, ancestors in the spiritual realm, still play a major role in the afffairs of the living. Guidance is sought from them through divination, enabling the living to interact with the spirit world.

Divination is usually done by a woman endowed with powers beyond those of ordinary men and women. This is a *sangoma* and she plays a prominent role in the daily lives of the Zulu.

Almost any bad thing in life is attributed to forces

beyond man's control, either witchcraft or offended spirits, but it is not beyond the intervention of the ancestors to intercede with the spirit world on behalf of the living and make life better for them.

Traditional religion was deeply entrenched in Zulu society for centuries and when Europeans introduced Christianity, the new faith did not find read acceptance among the Zulu and had difficulty gaining a foothold among them. And when it did, it was in syncretic form, with modification.

One of the most important figures in the history of the Zulu in terms of religion is Isaiah Shambe, considered a Zulu messiah, who merged Christianity with Zulu religion. He preached a form of Christianity which incorporated traditional religious beliefs into the new religion, a hybrid which found more acceptance among the Zulu than the teachings of Christianity introduced by Europeans did.

The Zulu also play a unique role in South Africa today. Although apartheid is now history, at least in the legal sense, and the all the people of South now have equal rights under the law, the Zulu have been a major opposition to the ruling African National Congress (ANC) since the end of white minority rule in 1994.

When the country was going through a transitional phase in the early 1990s, the Zulu demanded a federal form of government with extensive powers given to regional governments.

But they did not achieve their goal. However, they succeeded in defeating the African National Congress in elections in their home province, KwaZulu-Natal, and voted into office the opposition party, the Inkatha Freedom Party (IFP) which is, for a ll practical purposes, a Zulu party.

Many Zulus are also opposed to the ruling African National Congress (ANC) because they see it as a Xhosa party. In fact, the most prominent leaders of the ANC have been Xhosa. They include Nelson Mandela, Thabo Mbeki and his father Govan Mbeki, Walter Sisulu, Oliver Tambo, and Winnie Madikizela-Mandela.

Other prominent Xhosas are Robert Mangaliso Sobukwe, leader of the Pan-Africanist Congeress (PAC); Steve Biko, Bishop Desmond Tutu, Chris Hani, Mariam Makeba, and Hugh Masekela.

But simply because most of the most prominent leaders of the African National Congress during the struggle against apartheid and after the end of white minority rule were Xhosa does not mean that the ANC is a Xhosa party, whose detractors sometimes disparagingly refer to as La Xhosa Nostra.

One of the reasons a large number of Xhosas emerged as leaders of national stature during the struggle against apartheid and some of them eventually became national leaders after the end of white minority rule is that they were involved in the trade union movement and other activist organisations in relatively higher numbers than members of of other ethnic groups.

The most prominent Zulu of national stature is Jacob Zuma who once served as vice president under President Thabo Mbeki and was later elected the national leader of the ruling party, the African National Congress, in December 2007, paving the way for him to become the president of South Africa in 2009.

He also had overwhelming support among his people, the Zulu, in spite of their misgivings with the ruling ANC and remained solidly behind the Zulu-dominated Inkatha Freedom Party (IFP) led by Chief Mangosuthu Gatsha Buthelezi, a leader determined to preserve Zulu identity on the basis of regional autonomy within the context of South Africa as a single political entity. As he states:

"My party is committed to a federation....Personally, I believe in self-determination, but in the context of one South Africa - so that my self-determination is based in this region, and with my people....The IFP (Inkatha

Freedom Party) is here to put into practice what we preach.

All of our forebears contributed to what South Africa has become. That does not, however, mean that I must apologise to anyone for being born a Zulu, or for having that culture....

So long as the Zulu people are here, clearly I will still have a role to play in this country....

We have our own history, our own language, our own culture. But our destiny is also tied up with the destinies of other people - history has made us all South Africans." - (Chief Mangosuthu Gatsha Buthelezi, in *Mangosuthu Buthelezi Quotes*).

The Zulu are very proud of their culture and traditions and speak one of the most well-known languages in Africa and in the entire world.

The Zulu language is spoken by 24 per cent of South Africa's population as the first language. It is spoken by 10 - 11 million people, the Zulu, who also constitute about 24 per cent of the country's population. There are Zulus who live in Swaziland and in Lesotho as well as in other countries but most of them live in South Africa.

Smaller numbers of Zulus also live in Mozambique, Zimbabwe and Zambia.

Although the language is spoken mostly by the Zulu, about 50 per cent of the people in South Africa – including many immigrants and other foreigners – understand Zulu. Many of them also speak the language, some fluently.

Zulu belongs to the Nguni group and is a Bantu language like most in South Africa. And it shares a special characteristic and affinity with another language, Xhosa, which also belongs to the Nguni group and is a Bantu language like Zulu. The two languages – Zulu and Xhosa – are the only two languages in South Africa that are mutually understandable.

The correct name of the language among the Zulu

themselves is isZulu, although non-Zulus usually and simply call it Zulu.

The Zulu language evolved through the centuries by incorporating many sounds from the San and from the Khoi who are acknowledged as the first inhabitants of South Africa before a wave of Bantu immigration from the north swept across the region and supplanted them.

The clicking consonants in the Zulu language are clear evidence of their origin from the San and from the Khoi languages.

South African English has also incorporated a number of Zulu words into its vocabulary. The words *ubuntu* (humanity) and *indaba* (conference) are some of the examples. Others words of Zulu origin used in South Africa and elsewhere are i*mpala* and *mamba* (the snake – black mamba or green mamba).

It is one of the most widely used languages in South Africa because many people say it is not difficult to learn and it is easily understood.

Its sister language, Xhosa, is the second most widely spoken language, after Zulu, among many black South Africans.

It is spoken by about 18 per cent of South Africa's population. That's about 8 million people, mostly Xhosa. They are usually known as amaXhosa in South Africa and wanted to identified that way as a people. And their language is known as isiXhosa.

The Xhosa are closely related to the Zulu and migrated from the same region of the Great Lakes region in East and central Africa as the Zulu and other Nguni-speaking people.

Some of the ancestors of the Xhosa today arrived in what is now the Eastern Cape Province before the 1400s. And others came later in the 1500s and 1600s.

When they encountered the Khoi in the eastern Cape, conflict ensued in some cases, leading to the elimination and even enslavement of some of the Khoisan speakers.

But in general, the Khoi, also known as Khoikhoi, were absorbed and integrated into Xhosa society without ant problems.

Most Xhosas were cattle herders or farmers. Some were hunters. Besides maize, sorghum was another impotant crop as it is still today among the Xhosa. They also grew tobacco. Men also earned a living n the fields of woodwork and ironwork.

Tradititionally, Xhosa homesteads were organised on the basis of family ties and were patrilineal. The lineal descendants together with other related groups constituted the basis of the Xhosa social structure.

The building blocks of Xhosa society were also responsible for ensuring the survival and continuation of their bloodline by making sacrifices to the ancestors, by helping each other, and by carefully arranging marriages with neighbouring clans or lineages.

They are a heterogeneous group who have absorbed other groups through the centuries. Some of the most prominent Xhosa groups are the Pondo, or Mpondo, and Thembu both of which have produced prominent figures in South African history. Nelson Mandela came from the Thembu royal family, and Oliver Tambo came from the Pondo group as did Winnie Madikizela-Mandela.

The name Xhosa has an interesting origin. It does not come from Xhosa but from the Khoisan language and it means "angry men."

The Xhosa language is well-known for its click sound, a feature which make it difficult for many foreigners to learn although there are those who do. It has 15 different clicks, each with a different meaning.

There are other languages which also involve tongue-clicking, like Xhosa, and they are all of Khoisan origin. The Xhosa language is also representative of the South-western's Nguni family of languages and it's spoken everywhere in the Cape Province which is the native land of the Xhosa people.

There are also many Xhosas in the Western Cape Province and in Johannesburg and it's very common to hear them speak their language. There are also many Zulus in Johannesburg.

The Xhosa language is also spoken in Lesotho, Swaziland and Botswana, although in smaller numbers. And almost 45 per cent of all the people in South Africa speak Zulu, Xhosa, Ndebele or Swati as their first language. The rest speak other Bantu languages as well as others including English and Afrikaans as their native language.

Although the term Xhosa is commonly used by outsiders to identify a Xhosa or the Xhosa people, the appropriate term to identify a Xhosa, or Xhosas, is to use the term amaXhosa. Any amaXhosa man or woman will tell you that's the right term to use.

Like all the other black South African groups, the Xhosa have been in South Africa for a long time.

They migrated south probably from what is today the southern part of the Democratic Republic of Congo (DRC).

They travelled through central Africa and further down along the east coast until they arrived in the eastern part of the Cape. They settled in South Africa before the 1500s long before the white man arrived.

The first people the Xhosa came into contact with in South Africa were Khoisan-speaking people: the San and the Khoi, so-called Bushmen and Hottentots.

A lot of intermingling including intermarriage took place between them through the years. One of the most enduring results of this interaction was in the area of language.

The Xhosa borrowed many words including pronunciation from the Khoisan languages, as did the Zulu and other Bantu groups who migrated to South Africa, and this influence is clearly evident even today in black South African languages.

The click sounds of Khoisan languages are common in Xhosa, Zulu and other Bantu languages in South Africa. It is an enduring legacy, and that is why it is only the southern Bantu languages which have these sounds.

You don't find such sounds, for example, in Nyanja or Chewa spoken in Malawi, or in Nyamwezi and Hehe or Sukuma which are some of the native languages spoken in Tanzania, or in Bemba, the main indigenous language spoken in Zambia.

Many Khoisan-speaking people were also absorbed by the dominant Bantu groups through the years and became an integral part of those groups; the Zulu and the Xhosa being the most prominent. In fact one of the Xhosa clans, Gqunkhwebe, is of Khoisan origin. The Xhosa have a number of clans.

And physical features of the San and the Khoi are clearly evident among many Xhosas because of the intermarriage which has taken place through the centuries. One of the best examples is Nelson Mandela who, especially in his advanced years, clearly showed he had some of the facial physical features identified with the San and the Khoi, so-called Bushmen and Hottentots; so did Walter Sisulu from his mother's side – his father, a railway worker, was a white man of British origin.

So, there has been a lot of intermingling, including intermarriage, through the centuries among the Xhosa, as has been the case with other African groups, but as a people the Xhosa have maintained their identity as a distinct group and without compromising their essence.

When whites first settled in the Cape Province in the middle of the 17th century, the Xhosa were already living far inland and did not come into conflict with the white settlers until around 1770 when the Boers moved east – from the Cape in the west – towards Xhosaland.

Both the Boers and the Xhosa were stock-farmers and competition for land led to conflict between the two groups which culminated in a series of wars which went on for about 100 years.

As the colonial settlers became stronger, they started annexing land from the Xhosa. Annexation of land led to subjugation of the indigenous people – a policy pursued elsewhere with equally devastating results – and, by the middle of the nineteenth century, in the 1850s, almost all the land that had been inhabited by the Xhosa was under white control.

And during apartheid, the white government dominated by Afrikaners declared that the Xhosa would be confined to two homelands, or Bantustans, Ciskei and Transkei in what is now the Eastern Cape Province, a traditional Xhosa stronghold.

The Xhosa are closely related to the Zulu, the Swati, and the Ndebele; and so are their languages, of course. Their languages are mutually intelligible but they are considered to be separate languages mainly for cultural reasons because each group wants to maintain its unique identity.

There are political considerations as well, reinforced by ethnic pride and a sense of nationalism, derived from the fact that all these people separately constitute "nations," as they indeed were before they were conquered by Europeans and brought under one control.

In terms of life style, the Xhosa are mainly farmers and cattle owners like most black African groups whose languages belong to the Bantu family.

They are also the most southern group of the Bantu immigrants from Central Africa.

The Xhosa also have a very rich culture.

As in most parts of Africa, men play a dominant role in Xhosa society. And a boy becomes a man when his father determines that he is ready to go to the "hut".

He is set apart for a period of up to 6 weeks in which he is circumcised and taught the traditions of his people. Teaching ancestor worship is an important part of this time. This is typically done between 12 and 18 years of age. After this time, he is free to get married.

Marriages are arranged by the families. The family of the boy approaches the family of the girl and begins "negotiations". The *lobola*, or bride price, must also be agreed upon. It is typically 10 cows or the equivalent in money.

The bride is "captured" by the groom's family and taken to live with them; a practice also traditionally common among the Nyakyusa of Tanzania.

Among the Xhosa, traditionally, after the bride has been "captured," she and the groom are considered to be married. But if they are Christians, they go to the church for a two-day service in which one day is spent in the groom's village and the other in the bride's village.

Although Christianity and Western ways are no longer new among the Xhosa, ancestor worship still plays a very prominent role among the Xhosa.

Traditionally, hey believe the ancestors reward those who venerate them and punish those who neglect them. Many Xhosas mix ancestor worship with their Christian faith.

And there is a strong sense of loyalty among the people as members of the community or tribe. Most things are shared and those that have more are expected to share more. This is *ubuntu*.

The Xhosa are also well-known for their bead-work. Traditionally, their garments and ornamentation reflected the stages of a woman's life: a certain headdress was worn by a newly married girl; a different style by one who had given birth to her first child, and so on.

And Xhosa men traditionally fulfilled the roles of warrior, hunter and stockman; while the women looked after the land and the crops.

The land was communally held and great emphasis was placed on giving according to need. Everything was shared, in bad times as well as good. And Xhosa families still routinely help one another with such tasks as hut-building, a practice also traditionally common among some of the other African tribes.

Among the Nyakyusa of Tanzania, it was common even in the 1950s and 1960s among some people for a man to ask other men to come and help him build a house and even till the land, after which they feasted, eating plenty of food and drinking locally brewed alcohol called *ubwalwa*.

Tilling the land collectively, called *ndimila* in Nyakyusa, was highly functional and productive. It is also part of *ubundu*, as the Nyakyusa call it, and what the Xhosa and others in South Africa call *ubuntu*.

Also, traditional religion is central to life among the Xhosa and is one of the most powerful forces binding the people together. Legends of the Xhosa play the same role, also reinforcing their identity.

Xhosa legends or folklore have a lot in common with those of the other black African groups of Nguni origin such as the Zulu and Swazi.

Acknowledgement and recognition of the presence and power of the departed ancestors as an integral part of the living and of a Supreme Being, are basic elements of belief among the Xhosa.

Bad things which happen in life including illness are attributed to evil forces of supernatural origin; for example, *tokoloshe*, a hairy and potentially malevolent goblin who attacks at night.

Other entities include the huge lightning bird called *impundudu*, and the gentle *aBantu bomlambo*, supernatural beings in human form whom the Xhosa believe live in rivers and in the sea and who are said to accept into their family human beings who perish in the water, for example, from drowning.

Interestingly enough, the word *impundudu* is almost identical to the word *imbututu* the Nyakyusa of Tanzania use for a very large black bird. The difference is that while *impundudu* among the Xhosa is a large supernatural bird, *imbututu* in Nyakyusaland is natural bird.

And the term *imbututu* - also *mbututu* depending on the context in which the term is used if you know the Nyakyusa language as I do - is also used as a plural term. There are many such birds and they flock together.

I saw the birds myself in the 1950s and 1960s in Rungwe District, the homeland of the Nyakyusa, in Mbeya region in the Southern Highlands of Tanzania.

They were very large black birds with red beaks and they flew low every evening from a village called Nkuju to another village called Mpumbuli where they landed in some bushes not far from a river called Lubalisi which runs through that village.

The birds landed on a patch of land about 50 yards behind the family houses owned by two neighbours, Elijah Mwakikagile and Elijah Nsumbwe in Mpumbuli village in an area called Kyimbila about 4 miles south of the town of Tukuyu, the district headquarters of Rungwe District.

I saw those birds many times in that area and they made a lot of deep, low-pitched noise, singing in unison. Compared to the singing, or chirping, of other birds, that of the *mbututu* was like bass guitar.

I don't know the origin of the term *imbututu*, or *mbututu*, among the Nyakyusa, but the fact that these were very large birds – just as the *impundudu* is among the Xhosa – and their Nyakyusa name is almost identical to the one used by the Xhosa to describe a mystical bird in their culture, raises interesting questions in terms of common origin of many black African groups and their traditional beliefs.

It's very much possible that the term *imbututu* among the Nyakyusa also once referred to a mystical bird with supernatural influence in their lives, and the large black birds with red beaks they call *imbututu* or *mbututu* and which do exist in real life, remind them of that.

And among the Xhosa this huge, mystical lightning bird they call *impundudu* is as real in their traditional religious beliefs as the real, physical *imbututu* is among the Nyakyusa.

Such beliefs, deeply rooted in traditional religion, are common even today among most African tribes, although modernisation – which is mostly identified as a Western phenomenon of which Christianity and Western values constitute an integral part – has had a significant impact on some Africans who now shun those beliefs. Some do so only publicly while they continue to practise them privately.

Still, there is no question that traditional beliefs remain very strong and are central to the lives of the vast majority of Africans including those who have come under Western influence. The Xhosa are just some of those people.

Others include members of different tribes in Tanzania, besides the Nyakyusa, whom I have also included in this work for comparative analysis. As Sosthenes Mwita, stated in his article in the *Daily News*, Dar es Salaam, Tanzaania, 17 June 2008, entitled, "Rukwa Famous for Bizarre Cultures and Uncanny Superstition":

"Sumbawanga, the name of the administrative capital of Rukwa region, has an intriguing history. Though scanty and even hard to come by, available documentation dates back to 1914. Equally intriguing is the culture of the dominant tribe in Rukwa region – the Wafipa.

Before 1914 Sumbawanga was called 'Sumbu Wanga', which translates loosely to "discard your amulets" or "do not come here with fetishes of witchcraft," in the dialect of the highly superstitious Wafipa of the time.

A history booklet shows that the general fear among the Wafipa at that time was that some strangers could be better-skilled witchdoctors or magicians who could commit heinous atrocities given the chance.

The settlement's name appeared to warn strangers who had the temerity to come to 'Sumbu Wanga' against taking the 'offensive and diabolical' tools of their trade with them, lest they tangle with equally dangerous local magicians.

By 1929 the name of the settlement (Sumba Wanga) was adopted as the name of the administrative capital of the then Native African Authority. In 1950, the Ufipa District Council was installed.

However, as years rolled on, 'Sumbu Wanga' changed to Sumbawanga, the blame mainly coming from newcomers. By 1982 Sumbawanga town became a township through Act. No. 8 of the Local Government Authorities (LGAs).

The township had a population of 61,223 residents by then. Today, the Rukwa region has a population of 1,141,743 residents, going by the 2002 National Census and the forecast for last year was 1,349,749 people, according to National Bureau of Statistics (NBS) figures.

Major languages spoken in Rukwa region include; Kiswahili, Kifipa, Kimambwe, Kilungu, Kikonongo and Kinyamwanga. With the exception of Kiswahili, the other spoken languages are local vernacular. Other tribal settings in Rukwa include Wandende and Wapimbwe.

The main regional staple foods are mainly maize, rice and beans. In some parts of Lake Tanganyika and Lake Rukwa , cassava, fish and rice are the main source of food. Other food crops widely available include groundnuts, finger-millet and sweet potatoes.

The list of foods also includes round potatoes, sorghum, wheat and sugarcane. Meat is easily available from the pastoral communities that traditionally keep varieties of domestic animals such as cattle, goats, chicken, rabbits and pigeons. But rats and mice are also a favoured delicacy in some areas in Mpanda district.

The Wafipa, the largest tribal setting in Rukwa region, still have intriguing cultural norms and tenets of behaviour. Most Wafipa eat stiff porridge (ugali) cooked from finger-millet flour. Invariably, the ugali goes with beans or an occasional snack of rat or mouse meat popularly known as *koe*.

The Wafipa are hardworking farmers, who also grow maize, rice, groundnuts and sunflowers. Bumper harvests of maize and rice are a normal occurrence in Rukwa region. Nearly all Wafipa families use oxen-drawn ploughs to till the land.

Mr James Tuseko (71) an elderly man from the Wafipa tribe, says most households in his community raise an average of 12 head of cattle. However, most Wafipa, he says, do not drink milk. All milk is fed to dogs and house cats.

Among the Wafipa tribe, it is widely believed that witchcraft makers, mostly elderly men can make rain. The same miracle-makers can dispel or delay the onset of rain, according to Ms Wamweru Kataushanga, a rain-maker who has now laid down her tools.

The Wafipa are widely believed to be "very generous" people. However, some Wafipa men can be unforgiving if you steal or vandalize their property especially farm produce.

Wife-stealing is a cardinal sin that is punished heavily. An adulterous man who steals another man's wife is, consequently, hit by a powerful thunderbolt. The ominous signs of such an attack start with an insignificant gathering of rain clouds.

The resulting drizzle is said to be accompanied by thunder strikes, one of which hits the "wife-thief" with pinpoint precision, killing him instantly. Normally, the victim of such harsh punishment is one who has defied repeated warnings from the aggrieved husband.

Such weird punishments are believed to be meted out most prevalently in Nkasi district. Mr Tuseko says the man who suffered a similar fate was a police officer who had annoyed village elders

Mr Tuseko says the officer made frequent unwelcome visits on the fringes of Sumbawanga where he harassed villagers demanding favours corruptly, exacting torture and making arbitrary arrests.

He was, consequently, struck by lightning as he watched a game of soccer at a stadium. The bizarre aspect in this attack was that although the victim was seated in the middle of a thick crowd of spectators, he was the only one who was singled out for death.

Those seated close to him suffered minor burns and recovered after a few days. The Wafipa have a delightful dance called *nsimba*.

Ms, Nakama Nachirima (64) a former dancer, says music tools comprise two or three pots that vary in size; three-legged stools (one for each pot), a whistle and small stringed bells that are worn round the ankles. The pots are placed on the ground upside down, resting on their lids. The stools are placed on top of each upended pot. Skilled music makers twitch the stools in such a way that their legs tap on the pots, producing a scintillating rhythmical sound.

Each pot produces a different melodious sound, depending on its size. Women, mostly in Kitenge or khanga uniform, shake their shoulders, nod their heads and stomp their feet on the ground in tempo to the rhythm. In the heat of the moment, men join the fray.

The Wadende, who inhabit a portion of Mpanda district, are another tribal setting who has confounding culture. The Wadende are largely hunters and gatherers. They mainly thrive on meat, fruits and honey.

The Cultural Officer for Sumbawanga Rural district, Mr James Chelelo, says the Wadende are blamed for game hunting. "They mainly target small hoofed animals such as antelopes and gazelles," he says.

The Wadende live on the fringes of Katavi National Park where they hunt almost with impunity. Among the Wadende, each household owns a homemade gun. The Wadende are also skilled users of poison-tip arrows and spears.

According to Mr Chelelo, the Wadende till the land

albeit at a small scale growing maize and beans but their consumption of stiff porridge (ugali) is minimal. They also happen to inhabit mineral rich land, thus, some are small-scale miners.

The Wadende are also skilled beekeepers. It is uncommon to find a Wandende household which does not have a pot or calabash full of honey. Rukwa region came into being in 1974 when parts of Mbeya and Tabora regions were split to form a new region."

A lot of things the Wafipa and members of other tribes do in Tanzania – as well as in other parts of East, Central and Southern Africa – have striking similarities to what the people of black South African tribes do.

As in many other African tribes, the Xhosa in South Africa also have diviners.

A diviner plays many roles in Xhosa life besides being a traditional healer. A diviner also acts as an intermediary between the physical and the spirit world.

They are traditional doctors providing medicine, herbs and other traditional cures, for physical ailments. They also help people who suffer from mental and even provide psychological counseling in many areas. In Western medicine and health and mental care, diviner or traditional healer among the Xhosa and other African societies would be the equivalent of a conventional doctor, psychiatrist and psychologist – all rolled into one.

The diviners – or *sangoma* – among the Xhosa, the Zulu and many other black ethnic groups in southern Africa – are mostly women.

Among the Xhosa, they wear a shawl and headdress of fur most of the time. And they must undergo training under the guidance of a senior healer or healers before they start treating patients. It takes about five years working as an assistant to a diviner before you graduate and become one yourself.

Initiation rites differ in many ways between different

African peoples. One of the most common practices among many groups is circumcision. But with increasing urbanisation many groups have abandoned circumcision even though some individuals are circumcised for their own reasons including health.

Initiation takes many forms. Among the Xhosa, the youths whiten their bodies and wear a white blanket or sheepskin to ward off evil. During the ceremonies, enlivened by energetic dances, they wear costumes made from reeds, and at the end of the lengthy initiation period – spent in isolation from the rest of the community – the specially-built huts in which the young men have been living are ceremoniously burned.

Like most Africans across the continent, the majority of the Xhosa continue to live in the traditional way, and their tribal customs and traditions have remained virtually intact for centuries; as has their life style. Traditional mud-brick huts without running water or electricity still dot the hillsides, personal wealth is still measured primarily in terms of how many cows a man owns, and initiation of the youth into manhood is still common. Young boys going through their coming-of-age ceremony are called *abaKwetha*.

Maize is the main part of their diet. But they also eat a variety of foods. In many Xhosa homes, meals are accompanied by a traditional beer called *umquomboti*.

Music also is very important in the lives of the Xhosa. Some of the most internationally renowned musicians and singers are Xhosa. They include Miriam Makeba and Hugh Masekela.

Many Xhosas sing and dance to traditional music. Also a wide range of acapella and gospel choirs give regular performances on different occasions not only in Xhosaland in the Eastern cape Province but also in other parts o the country. They include Amatombazana, Black Mambazo, Bomvana Mamas, the Peace Brothers, and the Phandalwazi community choir.

And as a people, the Xhosa have had profound on South Africa throughout the nation's history. And they played a major role in the struggle for freedom from white minority which black South Africans endured for more than three centuries.

While the Zulu and the Xhosa constitute the two largest black African groups in South Africa, Afrikaners are the biggest group among South Africans of European descent. And their language evolved on African soil.

In fact, the majority of South African whites use Afrikaans as their first or second language. Even many blacks, including some leaders such as Nelson Mandela, speak Afrikaans.

Afrikaans is also widely spoken in Namibia and by a significant number of people in Botswana, Zimbabwe and other countries.

The name for the language, Afrikaans, is Dutch which means "African." It is also the first language among Coloureds who are a product of intermarriage.

The intermarriage took place among many groups. Immigrants from Indonesia and other parts of Asia as well as Madagascar intermarried with the Dutch and members of black African groups - especially the Khoikoi in the beginning in the Cape Province and later with others - to produce a distinct group of people known as Coloureds with their own unique identity.

And they have closely identified themselves with the Dutch culture – the culture of Afrikaners including the Afrikaans language – more than anything else in South Africa.

In fact 90 per cent of the Coloureds speak Afrikaans as their first language, contrasted with 60 per cent of whites who also speak Dutch. Therefore there are more Coloureds who speak Afrikaans as their first language than whites do. And whites who speak this language are mostly of Dutch origin.

Although Afrikaans is of Dutch origin in many

respects, it differs from Dutch in terms of grammar and vocabulary. It is, in fact, an African language in the sense that it was created on African soil, evolved on African soil, and has incorporated many words from black South African languages through the centuries.

The evolution of Afrikaans can be compared to that of Kiswahili, also known as Swahili, in some respects. Afrikaans is not a typical African language because a very large part of its vocabulary is of Dutch origin.

By remarkable contrast, Swahili is considered to be a "typical" African language because most of its vocabulary is African. Also its grammar and syntax is African. Yet, it is not a "typical" African language like Zulu or Shona or Kikuyu or Igbo or Yoruba or Ewe or Bemba because about 25 per cent to 30 per cent of its vocabulary is of Arabic origin.

Therefore it is also partly Semitic, just as Afrikaans – a language of Dutch origin – is partly African in terms of vocabulary, and in terms of evolution, of course.

Swahili also has borrowed a few words from Persian, Portuguese, Hindi, and German.

Arabic words in Kiswahili, or Swahili, include *raisi* (from *rais*), which means president; *waziri* (from *wazir*), meaning cabinet minister; *kahawa* (coffee), *sigara* (cigarette); *rafiki* (friend); numbers – *sita* (six), *saba* (seven), *tisa* (nine); *alhamisi* (Thursday), and many other words in different areas of life.

From Persian, Swahili has borrowed *chai* (tea), *diwani* (councillor), *serikali* (government), *achari* (pickle), and others.

Words of Portuguese origin in Swahili include *meza* (table) from the Portuguese word *mesa*; *pesa* (money) from *peso*; *leso* (handkerchief), *gereza* (prison); *sarafu* (currency – money), and others.

From English - *shati* (shirt), basi (bus), *baiskeli* (bicycle), *koti* (coat), and so on.

German contributions include *shule* (school), *hela*

(German coin) and others.

From Hindi, *chapati* and other words.

And that's not unusual for evolving languages to borrow words and even concepts from other cultures. English, the most widely spoken language in the world, has done the same thing. So has Afrikaans.

A very large part of the vocabulary of Afrikaans is of South-Hollandic Dutch origin. But Afrikaans also has many words from English, Khoi, San, Xhosa, Malay, Malagasy, Portuguese, French and German.

There are many other ethnic groups which are an integral part of South Africa.

One of the four major black ethnic groups in South Africa is the Venda; the other three being the Nguni (whose members include the Zulu and the Xhosa among others); the Shangaan-Tsonga; and the Sotho.

The Venda live mostly in Limpopo Province in the northern part of South Africa.

There are about one million Vendas and their language is also known as Luvenda, Tshivenda or simply Venda.

Their native land was once a Bantustan during the apartheid era in what was then the Transvaal Province before it became part of Limpopo Province after the end of white minority rule.

Although the vast majority of the Venda live in South Africa, a significant number of them also live in Zimbabwe just across the border. About 84,000 Vendas live in Zimbabwe, while the rest live in South Africa mostly in Limpopo Province. A significant number of them also live in the Northern Province.

As with most of the black South Africans, the Venda migrated south from the area of the Great Lakes region which includes the Congo.

They first settled in a mountainous area in the northern part of South Africa. The mountains in this part were later named Soutpansberg Mountains by the Dutch who ruled South Africa.

Their native land in this part – of South Africa and southern Zimbabwe – is a lush, mountainous and remote region; a factor that also explains why their culture, language, arts and crafts have remained virtually intact for centuries.

They have never been conquered by either the neighbouring tribes or the white settlers.

This is partly due to the remote country in which they live, and also because of the natural protection of the mountains to the south and east, with the Limpopo River shielding them to the north.

The Venda constructed permanent stone towns similar in style to Great Zimbabwe, which lies north of the Limpopo River over the border and is thought to have once been the capital of an empire that stretched across much of southern Africa – there is also a Venda minority in Zimbabwe.

The Venda built their first capital, D'zata, in that area and the ruins of this old settlement can still be seen today. The ruins are some of the most important historical treasures in South Africa.

The large walled city at Dzata was built in the 16th century, and there was a rich trade in ivory and slaves with the Arabs and Portuguese who were beginning to establish mercantile routes in the area.

The Venda first established the Mapungubwe kingdom in the northern part of South Africa in the 800s A.D. And their first king was Shiriyadenga.

The Mapungubwe Kingdom extended from the Soutpansberg Mountains in the south and across the Limpopo River all the way to Matopo Hills in what is now southern Zimbabwe, centuries before the Ndebele migrated north from South Africa and settled in this region which is now also known as Matebeland and part of the republic of Zimbabwe.

The Mapungubwe Kingdom gradually declined from

1240, and the centre of power and trade in the region moved north to the Great Zimbabwe Kingdom.

But in spite of the kingdom's decline, the Venda culture maintained its vitality. For example, south of the Limpopo River in South Africa, Venda and Shona-Venda pottery styles developed in the 14th and in the 15th centuries together with other cultural developments.

And although there are no stone-walled ruins in Limpopo Province comparable in stature and size to those of Great Zimbabwe in the northeastern part of the Northern Province (also of South Africa) there is definitely a strong cultural link between the two.

There was also a lot of intermingling between the Venda and the Shona. From around 1400, waves of Shona-speaking migrants from modern Zimbabwe - known by the Venda as Thavatsindi - settled across the Lowveld in South Africa, becoming an integral part of the communities in this region.

The Venda are generally regarded as one of the last black groups to have entered the area south of the Limpopo River.

Venda culture has retained its identity through the centuries. But it is also an eclectic mixture. There are many elements from the cultures of East and Central Africa. It also has some characteristics of Nguni and Sotho cultures. For example, the Venda practice male circumcision, which is common among many Sotho but not among most Nguni peoples. They also don't eat pork, a prohbition common among the people along the East African coast especially among Muslims.

Also British anthropologists Godfrey Wilson and Monica Wilson found out in their studies in the 1930s and 1940s among the Venda and the Nyakyusa of Tanzania, what was then Tanganyika, and of Malawi (then known as Nyasaland) that they shared a number of cultural characteristics.

Such similarities may indicate a common origin or

cultural interaction and exchanges between different African groups in the region.

The Venda language, TshiVenda or LuVenda, emerged as a distinct dialect in the 16th century. And in the 20th century, the TshiVenda vocabulary was similar to SeSotho. But its grammar shares similarities with Shona dialects which are spoken in Zimbabwe.

The Venda are also culturally closer to the Shona people of Zimbabwe than they are to any other South African group. Also, their language has a lot of similarities with Shona and Northern Sotho. It has also been influenced by the Nguni languages in some ways.

Venda culture has also been influenced by the Lemba, the black African Jews, who settled in the same region where the Venda live. The Jewish ancestors of the Lemba travelled from Yemen to what is now Tanzania and Mozambique before moving further south.

The beads they brought with them from these countries are still treasured to this day and are used in divination and other ceremonies. The Lemba are very good traders and artisans and are also famous for their metalwork and pottery, all of which has had significant influence on the Venda.

Another highly significant result of this interaction between the Lemba and the Venda is that many Vendas now also claim to have Semitic or Jewish roots. And that is because the Lemba have become an integral part of the Venda community, although it's a subgroup, within the larger community, which jealously guards its unique identity because of its Jewish heritage.

The Venda also prohibit their people from dealing with unclean animals such as pigs just as the Lemba do, and they don't eat pork just as the Lemba don't. Even the names of the two groups are similar: There's not much difference between Lemba and Venda. They sound basically the same.

The claim by the Lemba that they have a Jewish

heritage has been validated by science, including DNA tests done by South Africa's National Health Laboratory Services and the University of Witwatersrand in Johannesburg.

The scientists examined the Y chromosomes of the Lemba and found that 50 per cent were of Semitic origin, showing that the group originated in the Middle East around 1000 years ago.

Moreover, this particular type of chromosome found among the Lemba is a highly distinctive. It is the same chromosome found only in a hereditary Jewish priesthood sect known as the Cohanim. Inclusion into the sect was handed from father to son thus retaining the original Y chromosome, meaning that it is now scientifically proven that the Lemba, and therefore many Venda, are indeed descended from the ancient Israelites.

It has also been determined that the members of this sect of Jewish priests are descendanats of Aron, brother of Moses, in the Old Testament.

The Venda have also intermarried with the Tsonga, Lobedu, Zulu, Swazi and other people, all of whom have had significant influence on Venda culture.

Many of them also still practise polygamy and traditional religious beliefs in which departed ancestors play a central role.

Also traditionally, there is an important social division in Venda society between commoners, called *vhasiwana*, and the children of chiefs and their descendants who are known as *vhakololo*.

The Venda have a strong mystical tradition, and consider lakes and rivers to be sacred.

Water plays a very important part in the religious beliefs of the Venda and there are many sacred sites where the Venda consult their ancestral spirits.

In traditional religion, the Venda believe that water spirits known as *zwidutwane* live at the bottom of waterfalls. These supernatural beings are only half-visible.

They have one eye, one leg, and one arm. And this highly symbolic and of great religious significance in traditional worship aamong the Venda.

One half of these beings can be seen in this world and the other half in the spirit world. And traditionally, the Venda take offerings of food to them because the *zwidutwane* can not grow anything under water, in spite of their supernatural powers.

One of the most sacred sites of the Venda is Lake Fundudzi. There are many mythsa dn legends about the lake. It is fed by the Mutale River yet does not appear to have an outlet. It is also said that you can sometimes hear the Tshikona song although no one appears to be there. Tshikona is a Venda national dance.

The Venda are well known for their wood-carving, which has spiritual significance, and believe that the rains are controlled by the Python God, which lives in Lake Fundudzi.

Lake Fundudzi is consequently considered a sacred site, and visitors must obtain permission from the lake's resident priestess before approaching it.

In Venda folklore, the lake is home to huge python which is celebrated by young girls in the Venda fertility dance. The python is the god of fertility.

Lake Funduzi, in Thathe Vondo forest and surrounded by mountains, is also home to the mythical white crocodile; which might indeed have existed since the lake has many large crocodiles even today. And no-one is allowed to bathe or swim in the lake.

The *Domba* Python Dance is held one a year. An offering of beer is poured into the lake and as the final stage of their initiation into womanhood, Venda girls line up in a single file and dance in long winding lines like a snake.

The *Domba* is also very important in securing good rains for the following season.

Therefore one of the most important rituals among the

Venda is *Domba*, a pre-marital initiation.

It is also the last one in the life of a Venda girl or boy. The chief formally announces the beginning of a *Domba* and preparations are made by the families for their girls to be ready and to prepare what's necessary to attend the ceremony.

It is a rite of passage attended by both boys and girls who have previously attended other separate initiations for each gender, *Vusha* and *Tshikanda* for girls, and *Murundu* for boys when boys are also circumcised. The circumcision done during this rite was adopted from the North Sotho.

Only girls attend the *Domba* which has two main functions: teaching girls how to prepare themselves to become wives - birth planning, giving birth and child care, and how to treat a husband; and bringing fertility to the new generation of the tribe.

Many rituals are very special to the Venda and some of them are kept secret and not discussed with outsiders. But it is common knowledge that the python dance conducted at the female coming-of-age ceremony is usually where the chief chooses a wife.

Girls and boys dance fluidly, moving around like a snake, to the beat of a drum, while forming a chain by holding the forearm of the person in front.

And once a wife has been chosen, a number of courtship and grooming rituals take place during a period of a number of days.

The *Tshikona* is traditionally a male dance in which each player has a pipe made out of a special indigenous type of bamboo growing only in few places around Sibasa and Thohoyandou (which no longer exists). Each player has one note to play, which has to be played in turn, in such a way as to build a melody.

The *Tshikona* is a royal dance. Each ruler or chief has his own *Tshikona* band. *Tshikona* is played at various occasions for funerals, wedding or religious ceremonies.

In many important ways, it is indeed the Venda national dance or music, especially to the Venda who are indigenous to South Africa.

The *Tshigombela* is a female dance usually performed by married women. It is a festive dance sometimes performed at the same time as *Tshikona*.

There is another type of dance, *Tshifhasi*, which is similar to *Tshigombela* but it's performed by young unmarried girls who are known as *khomba*.

Drums are are very important in Venda culture. And there are legends and symbols linked to them. Most sets of drums are kept in the homes of chiefs and headmen and comprise one *ngoma*, one *thungwa*, and two or three *murumba*.

Drums are often given personal names and are always played by women and girls except in during some dances involving religious rituals when men may play them.

The Venda are known to be very artistic and produce many fascinating arts and crafts, with sculpture being particularly well-represented. Whether using wood or stone, the artist carves away the surplus material to reveal the true form or spirit of the object hidden underneath.

All this is easily dismissed by many people, especially Westerners, who see it as sheer superstition and witchcraft. But to the Venda, it is highly significant and central to their life and identity as a people. And it common among other tribes as well.

The Venda remain close to their ancestors through ancestral worship, and their art serves as a link and as a conduit to the world of spirits. Witchcraft is not viewed as an evil practice but a means to establish contact with the spirit world, usually when seeking guidance from the departed ancestors who remain an integral part of the living in almost every conceivable way.

Many Vendas go to traditional healers who diagnose their illnesses and then provide cures for them in consultation with the spirits in another realm which, despite its nature as an invisible world, is always inetricably linked with the physical world.

Ailments are cured or alleviated, for example, by making sacrifices and offerings, such as a chicken, to the ancestors and to appease the spirits. Herbs also are an integral part of the entire healing process, administered to those who have all kinds of physical, mental and even spiritual problems.

The Venda have maintained a solid traditional way of life, of which they are immensely proud, and continue to do so in spite of Western influence and modernisation which has spread in many parts of South Africa.

In the rural areas, cattle ownership is synonymous with wealth, and the lifestyle revolves around agriculture. Male and female roles are clearly defined, with the men responsible for livestock, ploughing and the building of huts, while the women do most of the harvesting as well as all the domestic duties.

Polygamy is still common, and due to the prosperity of the farmland, fewer men leave the area to work in the mines than is the case with many other tribes. As a result, traditional life has changed little over the years.

The Venda language is Bantu like all the other Black African languages spoken in South Africa except the Khoisan languages of the Khoi and the San.

And like all Bantu languages, Tshivenda is part of the Niger-Congo family which covers a vast expanse of territory stretching from Senegal in West Africa all the way to Kenya and Tanzania in East Africa and to central and southern Africa.

The Venda are some of the African people who continue to conduct their "national" life – as a Venda community – in the traditional way.

They have Tshivenda tribal councils of chiefs and elders who meet to discuss matters concerning their community, a form of government which is a practical alternative to western forms of government many African societies have adopted all the way down to the grassroots level with undesirable results in many cases.

Music is also very important in the Venda way of life, not only for entertainment but because of its cultural and religious significance and as a form of kinship binding the people together as a cohesive entity. It is an integral part of daily life among the Venda, unlike in many African societies across the continent where many people don't value music very much or as much as some members of different ethnic groups do.

The Venda have music almost for every event in their lives. There is music for worship. There is music for sadness.

The Venda also have music for work as many people of other African tribes do; for example, the Nyakyusa in Tanzania and Malawi who are said to share many cultural values and traditions with the Venda, according to the works of British anthropologist Monica Wlison who conducted her studies among the Venda and the Nyakyusa and other tribes in the region in the 1930s.

I remember witnessing this among the Nyakyusa in Rungwe District in the Southern Highlands of Tanzania in the late 1950s and 1960s. Many of them used to sing when they were working on their farms.

Also after work, many Nyakyusa, especially men, celebrate by drinking and singing at tradtional drinking places where locally brewed alcohol – mostly from maize and other grains – is sold. The Venda also, after working all day n the fields like the Nyakyusa, relax with traditional music, a few drinks and dancing.

I also witnessed funerals among the Nyakyusa which went on for days and where there was a lot of mourning and chanting, and quite often invoking the names – hence spirits – of the ancestors.

The invocation of ancestral names and guidance is an integral part of many African cultures.

Drum beating also is an integral part of most of the

music among the Venda. And a lot of their songs are usually murmured.

The Venda also have traditional meals just like other Africans do. And cooking is done the traditional way. The traditional meal among the Venda is Tshidzimba, a mixture of groundnuts, beans and maize or what's called *mielie* grains.

The term *mielies*, or *mielie-meal*, refers to maize. It's usually porridge and is a staple food among black South Africans. Another staple food among black South Africans is pearl millet.

The Ndebele are another Bantu ethnic group in South Africa who also live in southern Zimbabwe.

The Ndebele in Zimbabwe migrated from what is now KwaZulu-Natal Province in the 1830s. The fled from Zulu domination and encroachment by the Boers and established a new homeland in southern Zimbabwe. They are one of Zimbabwe's two ethnic groups – the other one is the Shona, the dominant group – and their homeland in southern Zimbabwe is known as Matebeleland.

They are members of the Nguni family of tribes. Altogether, the Nguni tribes constitute two thirds of South Africa's black population.

There are four Nguni groups: the Central Nguni, who are the Zulu-speaking people; the Southern Nguni, collectively identified as the Xhosa-speaking people; the Swazi people from Swaziland and adjacent areas; and the Ndebele of the Northern Province and Mpumalanga Province.

And there are some differences among the Ndebele themselves in South Africa, a product of historical, social and cultural circumstances.

The Ndebele in Limpopo Province as well as in the Northern Province and those in Mpumalanga Province have been separated not only by geography but also by differences in their languages and cultures.

The Ndebele in the Northern Province are mainly

members of the BagaLanga and the BagaSeleka tribes who very much have adopted the language and the culture of their Sotho and Tswana neighbours in this province. In fact, their language is sometimes mistakenly identified as a dialect of Northern Sotho because of the grat influence of Northern Sotho on this language. The younger Ndebele mostly speak Northern Sotho and their Ndebele language is gradually becoming extinct.

There are three groups of the Ndebele: the Southern Ndebele in Gauteng and Mpumalanga provinces; the Northern Ndebele in Limpopo and Northern provinces; and the Ndebele in southern Zimbabwe where they are also known as Matebele.

Unlike the Northern Ndebele, the Southern Ndebele have retain their unique culture and identity as a people. And they still speak "pure" Ndebele unlike their northern cousins.

The Ndebele people first moved away from their cousins, the Zulu, in KwaZulu and settled in the hills of Gauteng near the nation's capital Pretoria.

They were therefore an offshoot of the Zulu nation and left KwaZulu, or Zululand, in the 1820s under the leadership of Mzilikazi. They had the same skills of warfare their cousins, the Zulu, had and used them effectively across the Highveld against the Sotho and the Tswana whom they conquered. The Sotho and the Tswana were already living on the Highveld when the Ndebele arrived.

But when they attacked the Bosotho who lived in the mountains of what is now Lesotho, the former British protectorate of Basutoland, they were beaten back and settled in Western Transvaal.

The Ndebele tribe grew rapidly because they absorbed the people they had conquered and made them an integral part of the Ndebele ethnic group.

By 1835, they expanded their field of operations and were launching raids across a vast expanse of territory which included Swaziland and Northern Trasvaal.

But the region where they had established their stronghold, the Highveld, attracted the attention of the Boers because it was very fertile. The Boers, known as Voortrekkers, started moving into the region in 1836 in order to establish farms. And they were determined to oust the Ndebele from this region.

They attacked the Ndebele, and a series of bloody conflicts ensued. The first conflicts proved disastrous for the Boers. Several columns of the Voortrekkers were wiped out by the Ndebele. Then Mzilikazi launched a full-scale attack on a Boer stronghold at Vegkop on the Highveld but with disastrous consequences.

The Ndebele were no match for the Boers in terms of firepower; in fact, they had no guns and fought the Boers using traditional weapons. They were routed. The Boers were also helped by two African groups, the Griqua and the Tswana. The Ndebele fled to Northern Transvaal. But the Boers were not done with them and, under the leadership of Andries Pretorius, they attacked the Ndebele near a place that was later named after him – Pretoria – and forced Mzilikazi to go further north. Mzilikazi led his people and crossed the Limpopo River into what is now Zimbabwe. The Ndebele settled in the southern-western part of the country where they still live today.

Although the majority of the Ndebele under Mzilikazi moved north and settled in Zimbabwe, a significant number of them stayed behind in South Africa in the area around Gauteng Province. These are the Southern Ndebele who are now part of Mpumlanaga Province.

And despite the strong ties the Ndebele in Zimbabwe – known as Matebele – have with their kith-and-kin in South Africa, there are still some differences between the two because of the separation and different environments. For example, the Matabele do not paint their huts geometric patterns or wear neck rings; these are unique to the South African Ndebele.

The Ndebele also had their own problems before the Boers arrived on the Highveld and forced them to migrate farther north. When they arrived there, the Highveld was already inhabited by the Sotho and the Tswana.

The area where they first settled after they left Zululand became part of what later came to be known as the Transvaal Province after the Dutch extended their rule from the Cape and took the land away from them and the other indigenous people.

The Ndebele who settled on the Highveld split again years later, just as they had broken away from the Zulu earlier when they left Zululand.

Some remained on the Highveld which later became part of Transvaal – so named by the Dutch – and now the Northern Province after the end of apartheid, and came to be known as the Northern Ndebele.

The other group moved east and south and settled in what is now Mpumalanga Province and came to known as the Southern Ndebele. But in spite of the split, both groups remained distinctly Ndebele.

Even conquest by the Dutch did not succeed in destroying the cultural identity and unity of the Ndebele as a people.

Also the social structures and institutions of the Ndebele were similar to those of the Zulu, their cousins. The authority over a tribe was vested in the tribal head known as *ikozi* who was assisted by an inner or family council called *amaphakathi*.

Wards, known as *izilindi*, were administered by ward heads. And the family groups within the wards were governed by the heads of the families.

The residential unit of each family was called *umuzi* The *umuzi* usually consisted of a family head known as *umnumzana* with his wife and unmarried children. If he had more than one wife, the *umuzi* was divided into two halves, a right and a left half, to accommodate the different wives.

An *umuzi* sometimes grew into a more complex dwelling unit when the head's married sons and younger brothers joined the household.

Every sub-tribal group consisted of a number of patrilineal clans called *izibongo*. This meant that every clan consisted of a group of individuals who shared the same ancestor in the paternal line.

That was true in the case of the Ndebele as it was for the Zulu. And that is still the case today among the Ndebele and the Zulu who strictly follow their traditional way of life.

The lifestyle of the Ndebele, in terms of how individuals dress and portray themselves, has also persisted through the centuries. For example, Ndebele women traditionally adorned themselves with a variety of ornaments, each symbolising her status in society. After marriage, dresses became increasingly elaborate and spectacular.

In earlier times, the Ndebele wife would wear copper and brass rings around her arms, legs and neck, symbolising her bond and faithfulness to her husband, once her home was built for her.

She would only remove the rings after his death. The rings, called *idzila*, were believed to have strong ritual powers. Husbands used to provide their wives with rings; the richer the husband, the more rings the wife would wear.

Today, it is no longer common practice to wear these rings permanently but their cultural symbolism is still powerful in among the Ndebele and in Ndebele society.

In addition to the rings, married women also wore neck hoops made of grass called *isigolwani* twisted into a coil and covered in beads, particularly for ceremonial occasions.

Isigolwani are sometimes worn as neck-pieces and as leg and arm bands by newly-wed women whose husbands have not yet provided them with a home, or by girls of marriageable age after the completion of their initiation ceremony.

Married women also wore a five-fingered apron called *ijogolo* to mark the culmination of the marriage, which only takes place after the birth of the first child.

The marriage blanket called *nguba* worn by married women was decorated with bead-work to record significant events throughout the woman's lifetime.

For example, long beaded strips signified that the woman's son was undergoing the initiation ceremony and indicated that the woman had now attained a higher status in Ndebele society. It symbolised joy because her son had achieved manhood as well as the sorrow at losing him to the adult world.

A married woman always wore some form of head covering as a sign of respect for her husband. These ranged from a simple beaded headband or a knitted cap to elaborate beaded headdresses called *amakubi*.

Girls wore beaded aprons or beaded wraparound skirts from an early age. For rituals and ceremonies, Ndebele men adorned themselves with ornaments made for them by their wives.

Ndebele art has always been an important identifying characteristic of the Ndebele. Apart from its aesthetic appeal it has a cultural significance that serves to reinforce the distinctive Ndebele identity.

Ndebele artists also demonstrated a fascination with the linear quality of elements in their environment and this is depicted in their artwork. Painting was done freehand, without prior layouts, although the designs were planned beforehand.

The characteristic symmetry, proportion and straight edges of Ndebele decorations were done by hand without the help of rulers and squares. Ndebele women were responsible for painting the colourful and intricate patterns on the walls of their houses.

This presented the traditionally subordinate wife with

an opportunity to express her individuality and sense of self-worth. Her innovativeness in the choice of colours and designs set her apart from her peer group. In some instances, the women also created sculptures to express themselves

The back and side walls of the house were often painted in earth colours and decorated with simple geometric shapes that were shaped with the fingers and outlined in black.

The most innovative and complex designs were painted, in the brightest colours, on the front walls of the house. The front wall that enclosed the courtyard in front of the house formed the gateway, *izimpunjwana*, and was given special care.

Windows provided a focal point for mural designs and their designs were not always symmetrical. Sometimes, make-believe windows are painted on the walls to create a focal point and also as a mechanism to relieve the geometric rigidity of the wall design. Simple borders painted in a dark colour,lined with white, accentuated less important windows in the inner courtyard and in outside walls.

Contemporary Ndebele artists make use of a wider variety of colours (blues, reds, greens and yellows) than traditional artists were able to, mainly because of their commercial availability.

Traditionally, muted earth colours, made from ground ochre, and different natural-coloured clays, in white, browns, pinks and yellows, were used. Black was derived from charcoal. Today, bright colours are the order of the day.

As Ndebele society became more westernised, the artists started reflecting this change of their society in their paintings. Another change is the addition of stylised representational forms to the typical tradtional abstract geometric designs. Many Ndebele artists have now also extended their artwork to the interior of houses. Ndebele artists also produce other crafts such as sleeping mats and *isingolwani*.

Isingolwani, colourful neck hoops, are made by winding grass into a hoop, binding it tightly with cotton and decorating it with beads. In order to preserve the grass and to enable the hoop to retain its shape and hardness, the hoop is boiled in sugar water and left in the hot sun for a few days. A further outstanding characteristic of the Ndebele is their bead-work.

Bead-work is intricate and time consuming and requires a deft hand and good eyesight.

This pastime has long been a social practice in which the women engaged after their chores were finished but today, many projects involve the production of these items for sale to the public.

Although bead-work plays a very important role in Ndebele culture, it is an endangered art that is dying slowly. Western influence has had quite an impact on the Ndebele in some respects, leading to the erosion of their culture in some respects.

Bead-work is a vital component of Ndebele culture and identity. The most visible function of beads is body adornment and decoration of objects including clothing and ceremonial items. But they are used for more than that.

The beads are worn almost exclusively by women. And their different bead-work and beaded garments serve to identify their status from childhood to adulthood.

Bead-work is also an integral part of Ndebele rituals and ceremonies. There are rituals and ceremonies for important events in family life including birth, initiation of the youth into adulthood, marriage, and death with funerals accompanied by special ceremonies.

Working on beads is an arduous task. A bride may work for two to three years on a piece of bead-work she intends to present to the family of her future husband. And the more impressive it is, the more she will be admired and respected by her relatives-in-law and the community.

Also a woman may spend months and even years on intricate bead-work which will be used to adorn funeral garments. Such bead-work has religious significance because of the strong belief among the Ndebele that the dead continue to live in the next world which is the realm of spirits.

This highly impressive skill vital for such intricate designs is taught by mothers and passed on from generation to generation, with the daughters serving as the repository of knowledge in this field.

Their artistry of bead-work also has other uses: the painting of huts in geometric patterns. It is women who usually paint the huts and they draw inspiration from the intricate bead-work they wear. Much of their bead-work has bright polygonal patterns. Also integrated into the art are depictions of modern influence. For example, paintings of cars and other items of modern convenience are also included.

In Ndebele culture, the initiation rite, symbolising the transition from childhood to adulthood, plays an important role. Initiation schools for both boys and girls are held every four years.

During the period of initiation, relatives and friends come from far and wide to join in the ceremonies and activities associated with initiation.

Boys are initiated as a group when they are about 18 years of age when a special regiment called *indanga* is set up and led by a boy of high social rank. Each regiment has a distinguishing name.

Among the Ndzundza tribe there is a cycle of 15 such regimental names, allocated successively, and among the Manala there is a cycle of 13 such names.

During initiation girls wear an array of colourful beaded hoops called *izigolwani* around their legs, arms, waist and neck. The girls are kept in isolation and are prepared and trained to become homemakers and matriarchs.

The coming-out ceremony marks the conclusion of the initiation school and the girls then wear stiff rectangular aprons called *amaphephetu*, beaded in geometric and often three-dimensional patterns, to celebrate the event.

After initiation, these aprons are replaced by stiff, square ones, made from hardened leather and adorned with bead-work.

Marriages were only concluded between members of different clans, that is between individuals who did not have the same clan name.

However, a man could marry a woman from the same family as his paternal grandmother.

The prospective bride was kept secluded for two weeks before the wedding in a specially made structure in her parents' house, to shield her from men's eyes.

When the bride emerged from her seclusion, she was wrapped in a blanket and covered by an umbrella that was held for her by a younger girl who also attended to her other needs.

On her marriage, the bride was given a marriage blanket, which she would, in time, adorn with bead-work, either added to the blanket's outer surface or woven into the fabric.

After the wedding, the couple lived in the area belonging to the husband's clan. Women retained the clan name of their fathers but children born of the marriage took their father's clan name.

In traditional Ndebele society it was believed that illnesses were caused by an external force such as a spell or curse that was put on an individual. The power of a traditional healer was measured by his or her ability to defeat this force. Cures were either effected by medicines or by throwing bones.

All traditional medicine men and women called *izangoma* were mediums, able to contact ancestral spirits. Some present-day Ndebele still adhere to ancestral worship but many have subsequently become Christians and belong to the mainstream Christian churches or to one of the many local Africanised churches.

The language of the Ndebele people – who are also called amaNdebele and who call themselves that – is known as Ndebele or isiNdebele. And many people of other tribes in South Africa also speak Ndebele.

The Ndebele live in many parts of South Africa including Gauteng Province where their language and culture are clearly evident as in other areas of the country where they live in significant numbers.

There are more than half a million Ndebeles living in South Africa. Some Ndebeles also live in Botswana besides South Africa and Zimbabwe.

The Ndebele language is divided into two groups: Southern Ndebele and Northern Ndebele.

The people who speak Northern Ndebele live in and around Limpopo Province which was once known as Northern Transvaal.

Most of the people who belong to the Southern Ndebele group live in Mpumalanga and Gauteng provinces. Many of them also speak Zulu.

There are also a few words from Afrikaans and Northern Sotho (Sepedi) which have been incorporated into the Ndebele language.

And many young people, and even some older ones, who belong to the Northern Ndebele cultural and linguistic group also speak Northern Sotho which is the dominant language in Limpopo Province; it is also spoken in the North West Province. Northern Sotho is also known as Sepedi or Pedi, although Pedi is just one of the dialects of this language.

But the term Pedi has assumed greater significance and is used to identify the entire ethnic group of Northern Sotho.

Sotho speakers are the third-largest black African linguistic group in South Africa after the Zulu and the

Xhosa. There are about 7 million of them.

About 5.6 million Sotho live in South Africa, and 1.9 million in the small country of Lesotho which is completely surrounded by South Africa.

The Sotho are divided into three sub-groups. One of them is the Northern Sotho, also called Pedi or BaPedi. And their language, of course, is Sepedi, also known as Pedi or Northern Sotho.

The other two are the Southern Sotho, and the Tswana also known as BaTswana.

Like all the other Bantu-speaking groups in South Africa, the Sotho migrated from the Great Lakes region of East and Central Africa about 500 years ago. They moved south in waves of migration during different periods. The last group among Sotho to move south was the Hurutse who settled in Northern Transvaal towards the beginning of the 16th century.

It was this last Sotho group which eventually evolved into the Pedi.

Like most of the other black African groups in South Africa, the Sotho were traditionally farmers and cattle herders. They owned cattle, sheep and goats and grew maize, beans and other crops including tobacco. They were also well-known as craftsmen. They were renowned for their skills in metalworking, leatherworking as well as ivory and wood carving.

And like Nguni tribes, the Sotho also lived in small units under chiefs. But unlike the Nguni, the Sotho families lived collectively in villages and shared social and economic responsibilities for the entire community. Sotho villages were composed of wards, and each ward comprised members of more than one patrilineal descent group.

The position of chief was hereditary in Sotho society. And it was the chief who appointed the leaders of the wards whose homes were built around the chief's compound.

Sometimes, Sotho villages grew considerably and had thousands of people.

Their farms were usually some distance from the villages, and their clustered way of living – with many homes deliberately grouped together in villages – enabled them to defend themselves far better than they would have had they lived far apart from each other as members of other tribes did and still do. The consolidation of households into villages under the leadership of chiefs also enabled the leaders to effectively exercise control over their subjects.

The inhabitants of the villages were also divided into groups of men and women who were close in age. This is somewhat similar to what the Nyakyusa of Tanzania had: age villages. Young boys from the age of 13 would leave their parents' homes and start their own villages, get married, and build new communities.

The Sotho practice was not quite like that but the age-sets in their villages had specific responsibilities just as young Nyakyusa boys had a responsibility to establish their own villages and start families independent of their parents.

Among the Sotho, the men, depending on the age group to which they belonged, acquired skills in warfare and taking care of domestic animals especially cows; while women learnt how to take care of crops and fulfill a number of religious responsibilities.

Usually, a whole group of young men or women who were close in age moved from one task to the next, after mastering the skills, and the people in the village community marked this transition with celebration involving rituals and sometimes an initiation ceremony, a practice honoured for generations.

Although both the Sotho and the Nguni have patrilineal descent, their marriage customs are different in some important respects.

Traditionally, the Sotho practise endogamous marriage,

marrying within the group, and prefer marriage partners to whom they are related through patrilineal descent ties; while the Nguni – among them the Zulu, the Xhosa, the Ndebele and others – practise exogamous marriage and prohibit marrying anyone within the descent group.

The Sotho came under increasing pressure from white encroachment and were eventually overwhelmed just like all the other black African ethnic groups were. They lost most of their land, putting a severe strain on them; a far cry from what they were in the past before they were conquered by the white man.

Their society was originally a confederation of small chiefdoms which had been established before the 17th century in what came to be known as Northern Transvaal, now the Northern Province.

The Pedi also suffered at the hands of the Ndebele and the Boers. In the 1830s, they were attacked by the Ndebele who were led by Mzilikazi and lost the war.

And during the second of the 19th century, during and after the 1850s, they had a number of clashes with the Voortrekkers, the Boers who had moved north from Cape to found a new colony, the Transvaal. Later in the 1870s, they clashed with the British who had taken over the Transvaal from the Boers, becoming the new rulers.

And in spite of the crushing defeat they suffered under the Ndebele whose reign of terror under Mzilikazi spread throughout Northern Transvaal, wreaking havoc, the Pedi regrouped and survived as a people and as an ethnic entity of the Sotho.

Although the Pedi were of Sotho origin, their intermarriage with members of other tribes – whom they defeated in war - led to incorporation of many words and customs into Pedi language and culture from those tribes. The words which became part of the Pedi vocabulary came from the Venda, the Lovedu, and the Karanga of what is now Zimbabwe. Also many customs came from those tribes and were not of Sotho of origin.

The social and cultural life of the Pedi has been shaped by their traditions and customs for generations.

Traditionally, the Pedi live in round-shaped huts. The clay used to build the huts is mixed with cow dung to strengthen it. Cow dung is known as *boloko* in their language.

The practice of using cow dung mixed with clay is used by other African tribes in building houses. For example, the Nyakyusa of Tanzania also traditionally used cow dung, called *ndope*, mixed with clay, known as *matope* in Nyakyusa, to build their houses. Decoration of the houses was done by rolling a corn cob on the wet walls, creating a pattern.

Bt with modernisation, the practice has largely been abandoned by the Nyakyusa. However, there are those who still do that just as the Pedi do.

Among the Pedi, the roofing of their traditional round huts is made from a particular kind of grass called *loala* which is long and strong. Members of other African tribes do basically the same thing. The Nyakyusa also use grass, called *ilisu*, for roofing. Traditionally, the Nyakyusa build rectangular houses, not huts.

The Pedi have a variety of traditional foods. They include *thophi* made from maize mixed with a fruit called *lerotse*; and *morogo wa dikgopana*, which is cooked spinach that's shaped round and left in the sun to dry up. They also use milk and vegetables, among other foods.

The traditional religion of the Pedi involves intercession with the gods by departed ancestors who represent the living in the realm of spirits. They also have initiation rites for boys and girls in their transition from childhood to adulthood.

They also have a code of ethics which they enforce by ostracising or banishing from the village anyone who violates their culture.

The Pedi also have arranged marriages, with the elders choosing spouses for their sons and daughters. The bride's parents determine the dowry, usually cows but also money. The dowry is called *bogadi*.

Their culture also allows younger brothers to marry the widows of their dead elder brothers; a custom the Pedi justify by saying it's necessary in order to support the family and take care of the children.

And when a baby is born to a chief, the villagers go to the chief's residence, called *moshate*, to give presents to the child and wish the baby well. A few days after that, the chief's subordinates announce that a ceremony will be held on a certain day for the whole village. The villagers gather to sing, dance and feast on traditionally prepared food and drinks to celebrate the birth of the chief's child.

Singing and dancing is a very important part of Pedi culture. For example, the people sing when they have hard work to do in order to "finish" the job quickly and for encouragement. They also sing on other occasions.

The Sepedi language, or Northern Sotho, is also known as Sesotho sa Laboa. In South Africa, the language is spoken by more than 4.2 million people and most of them live in Gauteng, Mpumalanga and Limpopo provinces. Sepedi is also spoken in Botswana by a few people.

Northern Sotho (Sepedi) is very closely related to the Setswana and Sesotho languages. The people themselves are closely related although there are some differences in culture and tradition. But even in these areas, there a lot of similarities among them.

These similarities also transcend national boundaries which were drawn by the Europeans when they conquered Africa.

The wedding ceremonies of the Sepedi have a lot of similarities with the wedding ceremonies of the members of many other African tribes; for example, the Nyakyusa of Tanzania and Malawi whom I have used for comparative study in this work which focuses on South Africa and its people.

Among the Sepedi, or Northern Sotho, the bride and

the bridegroom's closest and senior family members get together to discuss the wedding including the dowry. The Nyakyusa of Tanzania and Malawi do basically the same thing.

The Sepedi (Northern Sotho) call dowry – *lebola*. The Nyakyusa call it *lobola*.

The Zulu and the Xhosa also call it *lobola* just like the Nyakyusa do. The Swazi call it *lobolo*.

They are all basically the same words, linguistically, and they all mean the same thing: dowry.

Also among the Sepedi and the Nyakyusa, it is usually the bride's parents who decide what kind of dowry should be demanded. Among the Nyakyusa, it is usually cows; and among the Sepedi, it is also usually livestock and even money or it can be anything.

Among the Zulu, the father and uncles of the bride decide what the dowry should be, and what items should be given to the bride's family as *lobola*.

If the bridegroom's parents refuse to "pay" that, the bride is not going to be given to the prospective husband by her parents. There will not be any wedding. But usually a compromise is reached and the bride is given away by her parents.

This is common practice among the Sepedi, the Nyakyusa and many other African tribes or ethnic groups in different parts of the continent.

A Sepedi wedding is usually held at the bride's or bridegroom's home. Among the Nyakyusa, traditionally, it is held at the bridegroom's home not at the home of the bride. So there are some differences, but not fundamental, and not in terms of formalities in general.

Also among the Sepedi, when the bride is dressed and ready for her wedding, she is required to go to the river and draw enough water and collect some firewood for the ceremony. The Nyakyusa don't do that.

After a Sepedi bride has collected enough water and firewood and has fulfilled other tasks on the day of the wedding, she's ready to walk to her future husband during the ceremony, while her grandmother sweeps the floor in front of her to "clear her way."

The Nyakyusa don't do that, either, but the bride's mother and other female relatives are always there, at a Nyakyusa wedding, to "escort" the bride or their daughter, accompanied by *akalulu*, as the Nyakyusa call it, which is making joyous sounds at a high pitch and with the rapid movement of the tongue hitting the cheeks inside, back and forth, to accentuate the rhythm.

Such ululation by the women, which is an integral part of Nyakyusa culture, is common in other African societies as well.

Among the Sepedi, after the couple is married and the people at the wedding have congratulated them, a cow or a sheep is slaughtered and the meat is equally divided between the two families.

The Nyakyusa do basically the same thing but the food and the drinks brought to the wedding ceremony are consumed by the people who are at the wedding. And some of it is, of course, shared between the families of the bride and th bridegroom' which is not very much different from what the Sepedi (Northern Sotho) do in their culture at weddings.

After the wedding has formally taken place, the Sepedi celebrate with music, what they call *kiba*. And only men are allowed to dance to *kiba* music, a cultural restriction that is not imposed on the people in all African societies, although the Sepedi, or Northern Sotho, may not be unique in this regard.

One of the ethnic and linguistic groups which transcends national boundaries is Setswana.

The Tswana or BaTswana are inextricably linked with the Northern and Southern Sotho in terms of origin and are sometimes known as the Western Sotho. And their language is closely related to SeSotho or Sotho, which is Southern Sotho. In fact the two languages are mutually intelligible in most areas.

The Tswana migrated from East Africa around the same period when other people left the region and moved south, eventually settling in southern Africa.

There are about 4 million Tswana in the countries of southern Africa. About three million of them live in South Africa, and 1 million in Botswana. There are smaller numbers in other countries such as Lesotho, Namibia, and Zimbabwe.

In South Africa, many Tswanas live in the areas that once collectively constituted the Bantustan of Bhophuthatswana during apartheid. They also live in the neghbouring areas of the North-West Province and the Northern Cape Province. Many of them also live in cities and towns throughout South Africa but the majority of the Tswana live in the northeastern part of South Africa adjacent to their kith-and-kin, the Tswana, in the country of Botswana.

Bhophuthatswana was a patchwork of scattered territory – seven pieces of land – in the former South African provinces of Cape Province, Transvaal and Orange Free State. The capital Mmabatho was located in an area bordering Botswana. It was established to accommodate the Tswana in South Africa and had a population of about 1.8 million people in the late 1980s, more than 15 years after it was established as a homeland in 1971.

The population was about 70 per cent Tswana in the late eighties. The rest were other Sotho people as well as Xhosas, Zulus and Shangaan. And another 1.5 million BaTswana lived in different parts of South Africa besides Bhophuthatswana.

After apartheid ended, five of its enclaves became part of the North West Province; one part was integrated into the Free State Province, and the remaining enclave became part of Mpumalanga Province. And its capital Mmabatho became the capital of the North West Province.

And in spite of the integration of the enclaves into the

new provinces, those areas remain Tswana strongholds because they were already the traditional homes of the Tswana even before the apartheid regime grouped them together to create the Bantustan of Bhophuthatswana.

The Tswana have had a turbulent history mainly because of the clashes they had with other African groups, especially the Ndebele on the Highveld, and with whites who moved into the same region to seize land from blacks indigenous to the region.

By the 19th century, several Tswana groups were politically independent. But they were also loosely affiliated chiefdoms and clashed with the Boers many times when Afrikaner farmers demanded land in the northern part of Transvaal whee the Tswana lived.

And towards the end of the century, the Boers and the British seized almost all the land that belonged to the Tswana, forcing them to become migrant labourers working especially in the mines for very low pay.

The culture of the Tswana is closely related to the cultures of the Sotho, with whom they are related. They share a lot of similarities in language, customs, religion, social and political organisation, family life, and claim a common ancestor: Mogale.

But there are some notable differences. For example, Tswana chiefdoms were traditionally more stratified than those of the other Sotho – they are Sotho themselves - and of the Nguni groups such as the Zulu, the Ndebele, and the Xhosa.

The Tswana also had a highly complex legal system, with courts ranked from the lowest to the highest. Their legal system also included mediators. And those found guilty were given stiff punishment.

They also had very close working relationships with their neighbours, the Khoisan-speakers who were hunters and herdmen, with whom they conducted barter. As hunters, the Khoi provided the Tswana with meat and animal pelts and, in return, they got cattle from the

Tswana. And they sometimes got dogs from the Khoi and used them for herding cattle.

The Setswana language is commonly known as Tswana. And it is the national language of Botswana because about 98 per cent of the people in Botswana are Tswana.

But the majority of the Tswana and speakers of Setswana live in South Africa. That is where the Tswana in Botswana came from.

The majority of the Setswana-speaking people in South Africa live in the Northern Cape Province which once was part of the Cape Colony. The Cape Colony was later remaned the Cape Province. And it was the largest among the four provinces which constituted South Africa during the era of white minority rule. The other provinces were Orange Free State, Transvaal, and Natal.

Internationally, there about 4 million Tswana speakers. Tswana speakers also live in Zimbabwe and Namibia. But they are all outnumbered by those who live in South Africa. Before the end of apartheid, the Tswana in South Africa were given their own homeland, Bophuthatswana, as an "independent" state by the apartheid regime.

Tswana is a Bantu language most closely related to Northern Sotho and Southern Sotho.

The Tswana people have a lot in common with other black South Africans and other Africans elsewhere on the continent in terms of culture.

Cattle are an integral part of life among the Tswana and cattle ownership symbolises wealth; the more cows you have, the wealthier you are. The same standard of measurement is applicable in other African cultures as well.

Also traditional healers known as *sangoma*, and music, play very important roles in the lives of the Tswana; common phenomena in other African societies.

The traditional religious belief of the Tswana acknowledges the existence of a Supreme Being. It is therefore monotheistic and predates the introduction of Christianity to Africa in its conception of one God.

Modimo is the "Great Spirit," the great God, one God. And intercession by departed ancestors on behalf of the living is just a way to reach the Creator for his guidance and blessings in temporal life which includes spiritual growth.

The other Sothos – Southern and Northern – also worship *Modimo* in their traditional religion.

The departed ancestors are called *balimo* and they are honoured at ritual feasts. Misfortune including sickness is bound to occur if you incur the wrath of the ancestors, *balimo*, who are the ones who can seeking blessings from *Modimo* for the living.

The Southern Sotho are a heterogeneous group and were once united in the 1830s under the highly efficient leadership of King Moshoeshoe who also had a reputation as a skilled diplomat. He was originally a local chief but became king after uniting various ethnic groups under his leadership to maintain and secure their freedom and resist Zulu encroachment.

Moshoeshoe united people of different ethnic groups who had fled from invasions by the Zulu under Shaka and sough sanctuary in the mountains of what is now the country of Lesotho. They included groups of Sotho speakers and the Nguni, all of whom had been uprooted by the *mfecane*.

Some of the fleeing groups established ties with the San who lived just west of Moshoeshoe's kingdom. The ties led to a lasting relationship and cultural exchanges which are clearly evident even today in the language of Southern Sotho which uses click sounds unlike Northern Sotho. The clicks came from the Khoisan languages and have been incorporated into the languages of other black African groups in South Africa including the Xhosa and the Zulu.

During apartheid, the Southern Sotho were given the

tiny homeland of QwaQwa in the early seventies located in the eastern part of the former South African province of the Orange Free State bordering Lesotho in pursuit of the government's policy of racial separation. About 200,000 Southern Sotho lived in the homeland during the 1980s. And after apartheid ended, the Bantustan was incorporated into the Free State Province.

The language of Southern Sotho, which is closely related to Setswana and is twin to Northern Sotho, is also known as Suto, Souto, Sisutho and Suthu.

Although Southern Sotho, Northern Sotho and Setswana are closely related, they are still considered to be separate languages.

Southern Sotho is also the main language spoken in the country of Lesotho, and most of the people in Lesotho are Southern Sotho.

It is one of the two official languages – the other one being English – in Lesotho and is spoken by more than 90 per cent of the people in this country which is entirely surrounded by South Africa.

Southern Sotho is also spoken by some people in Botswana, Namibia and Zambia.

And in South Africa, the majority of the Southern Sotho live in the Free State Province which borders Lesotho on the west. Also a significant number of them live in other provinces, especially in towns and cities.

As in all African cultures, respect for elders is extremely important among the Sotho. And in Southern Sotho language, the words for father and mother – *ntate* and *mme*, respectively – are also used to address elders including non-relatives and strangers, and not just one's parents and relatives, to show respect for them.

Traditionally, the Sotho have always valued arranged marriages, a practice that was common among many other African tribes including the Nyakyusa of Tanzania and Malawi - but many young men and women now have more freedom to marry whom they choose.

The traditional way of life is centred on villages ruled by chiefs. And livestock, especially cattle, and farming are the most important sectors of the economy in the Sotho traditional society. Main crops include maize and sorghum.

The Sotho have initiation rites for boys and girls. They are critical in the traditional way of life and ensure passaged from childhood to adulthood.

During the initiation period, boys are required to stay in a secluded place away from the village. They are circumcised, taught traditional praise songs, and the proper way to be men and husbands as well as to be responsible members of the community. They also learn tribal traditions dealing with initiation.

At the end of the initiation period, ceremonies are held during which the newly initiated called *makolwane*, who are now no longer "boys" but responsible adults, sing the praise songs they composed when they were going through initiation.

The Sotho believe that a man who has not been initiated is not a full adult and still belongs in the same category as "boys," even not quite so in the literal sense. Few men, if any, want to subject themselves to such indignity.

For the girls, who are called *bole* when they are going through initiation, the rite of passage involves seclusion. But the huts in which they are kept are much closer to the villages than those for boys are.

The girls wear masks and smear their bodies with a chalky white substance and are sometimes seen near the homes of their relatives, singing and dancing, and asking for presents.

After the seclusion period is over, the newly initiated, who are now no longer girls and are called *litswejane*, anoint themselves with red ochre and wear traditional skirts. But they don't undergo circumcision during initiation as boys do.

Among the Southern Sotho in Lesotho, initiation for

boys or young men took another dimension when they incorporated one aspect of modernisation into it. For Sotho men who worked in the mines, the period they spent as mine workers was once considered as a rite of passage into adulthood.

Ethnic ties among the Sotho are very strong; so is adherence to customs and traditions demonstrated, for example, by the way funerals are conducted. When a person dies, the whole community gets involved in the funeral. Friends and relatives give speeches at the graveside before the burial takes place, honouring the deceased and bidding him or farewell, and adult men take turns shovelling soil into the grave.

After the burial, all those who attended the ceremony go as a group to wash their hands. There may even be funeral feast in the end.

Ubuntu is also one of the strongest characteristics of traditional Sotho society. The hungry, including strangers, are never left alone. Even the poorest feel morally bound to share what little they have with someone who comes to their door. That is *ubuntu*, one of the most important principles in traditional African society. It is a philosophy and a way of life.

Although arranged marriages have been an integral part of the Sotho way of life for generations, if not for centuries, most young men and women nowadays marry the person they want to marry. Before then, arranged marriages extended even to children. A girl could be betrothed in childhood - when she did not even the slightest idea of what marriage meant.

As in most traditional African societies, a man is th head of the family. Women take care of the crops and responsible for bringing up children.

Family responsibilities are based on gender but the Southern Sotho differ somewhat from their kith-and-kin, the Pedi or Northern Sotho in some respects. For example, the Northern Sotho are much more stricter than the

Southern Sotho in maintaining separate living spaces for men and women.

Polygamy is still practised, especially for those who can afford it. And when conducted in the traditional way, marriages are arranged by transferring dowry, called *bohadi*, from the bridegroom's family to that of the bride. And after marriage has taken place, a woman is expected to leave her family to go and live with the family of her husband. It is now their – especially the husband's – full responsibility to take care of her.

Traditionally, the Sotho have a unique way of maintaining kinship through the generations. A person is allowed to marry a cousin - *ngwana wa rangoane* - who is a member of the same clan.

In terms of traditional attire, the Southern Sotho – in Lesotho for example – are known for their brightly coloured blankets.

They don't make them but buy them from modern shops in towns. And the blankets keep them warm during winter, especially in mountainous Lesotho, a country located high up in the Drakensberg Mountains.

The most important part of their diet is maize. They also eat a variety of meat and vegetables. Milk is often drunk in soured form, a common practice among other tribes including the Xhosa and the Zulu, and the Nyakyusa in Tanzania. The Nyakyusa call "milk" - *ulukama* or *lukama*, depending on the context in which the word is used.

Music also is a very important part of Sotho culture. While in many societies people sing as individuals, among the Sotho a strong emphasis is placed on singing in groups. And dancing is usually accompanied by hand clapping.

The Southern Sotho have produced one of the earliest and most distinguished writers in African literature. His name was Thomas Mofolo and one of his first novels in a South African language was *Chaka* published in early part of the 20th century. It is still read today and has been translated into many languages.

The Sotho are also known for their bead-work, pottery making and weaving, traditional skills which have been handed down through the generations and which remain one of the most important aspects of many traditional African societies.

Many items, for example, baskets, sleeping mats and beer containers, are still woven by hand from grass materials and are common among the Sotho in Lesotho and South Africa.

The Southern Sotho have been greatly influenced by other cultures in some very important ways. One of those lareas is language.

The Sotho language, which is one of the 11 official languages of South Africa, has been influenced by Khoisan languages and uses click consonants in some words, a feature adopted from Khoisan languages and not found in typical Bantu languages.

The Sotho have played a significant role in the history of South Africa and Lesotho and are one of the most well-known ethnic groups in the entire region of Southern Africa.

Another Nguni group which settled in South Africa centuries ago in the Swazi. And their language, Swati, is one of the 11 national languages of South Africa. It is also spoken in neighbouring Swaziland where the Swazi constitute the majority of the population.

There are more than 1.6 Swazis in southern Africa. About 900,000 of them live in the small country of Swaziland which borders South Africa. And the rest live in South Africa especially in KaNgwane, adjacent to Swaziland, which was designated as their homeland by the apartheid regime.

The Swazi migrated from east-central Africa in the 15th and 16th centuries together with the Xhosa and the Zulu and settled in the southern part of the continent.

They were part of the Nguni wave of migration from the north and after they crossed the Limpopo River, they settled in southern part of Tongaland in what is now Mozambique in the late 1600s.

After 200 years, the Swazi moved into the region on the Pongola River where they lived in close proximity to the Ndwandwe people who were Zulu.

Later on, land shortage and other problems sparked a conflict between the two groups, forcing the Swazis to migrate to the central area of what later became the country of Swaziland.

From that central region, they continued to expand their territory and jurisdiction by conquering numerous small Sotho and other Nguni groups.

The area they claimed was twice the size of modern Swaziland. Many Swazis also settled in South Africa.

Many Swazis who were forced out of South Africa by the Zulu went even further north, together with some Zulu clans who also had been uprooted by Shaka's successors, and established control over some tribes in regions which later became the countries of Nyasaland, Southern Rhodesia and Northern Rhodesia, now renamed Malawi, Zimbabwe and Zambia.

The name Swazi comes from the name of their ruler, King Mswati, and simply means the people of Mswati. As a people they are also called BaSwazi.

Traditionally, the Swazi are subsistence farmers and cattle herders – they also own goats but mostly cattle – but a significant number of them are part of the urban economy because of modernisation.

The Swazi way of life is essentially traditional in most fundamental respects including religion. Most of them are Chrsitian but probably the majority of Swazis, even many Christians, still consult traditional healers.

A significant number of them have adopted Western ways and embraced modernisation. Still, even among these, traditional values and customs play a major role in their lives.

The extended family, an integral part of the social fabric remains strong, and many people still believe in polygamy even if they have embraced Christianity.

Traditional music and dance are an integral part of Swazi culture. The Swazi are also known for praise-singing. They compose praise-songs for their king, for their chiefs and other prominent people they want to honour. The Swazi also have music for marriage, harvest, funerals and other important events.

Some of the most important ceremonies among the Swazi in Swaziland are *inkwala* and *umhlanga*. Both are traditional dances with great cultural significance.

Inkwala is a "Festival of the Fruits" ceremony. It's held in the latter part of December and continues into January in the following year.

It is the most sacred, and most important, ceremony among the Swazi and all the people, especially male, converge at the royal kraal for several weeks of traditional dancing where they are joined by the king.

It is an annual ceremony lasting three weeks that unites the inhabitants of Swaziland in order to gain blessings from ancestors. This important event also serves the purpose of renewing the kingship of the nation and commencing the harvesting season.

Inkwala involves sacred and secret ceremonies whose details are kept secret to protect their integrity.

The ceremony is also very important to the Swazi who live in South Africa as much as all the other traditional Swazi ceremonies are, regardless of where they performed because of the identity of the Swazi as one people.

Umhlanga is the "reed dance." It's held in late August or early September.

The "reed dance" has been an integral part of the traditional way of life for a very long time and it's held in August or early September because of the weather. It's warm and sunny. This is also the period when the reed has matured.

Up to 30,000 maidens congregate and dance for the public. They come from all parts of Swaziland to participate in the dance. The dance is also highly significant among the Swazi in South Africa because of the ethnic and cultural bonds the people share. They are all Swazi.

The reed dance is also performed by the Zulu in KwaZulu-Natal Province. In fact, the term *umhlanga* is both Zulu and Swazi and refers to the common reed.

The tradition of the reed dance was to encourage young women to abstain from sexual activities and preserve their virginity until they were mature enough to get married. It also prepares the girls for marriage.

During their stay at the camps before the actual dance, they are given certain tasks to perform in groups. There is a lot of group work involved and, because of that, the girls also get the chance to improve their communication skills which will help them in solving some of the problems they will face in marriage.

There are also elder women at the camps who advise the girls on marriage-related subjects and on how to handle themselves in a dignified manner.

The night after the girls arrive at the camps and after they have eaten supper, they girls walk to a place where they are pick the reed.

It is a long distance from the camps and the trip may take the whole night. But this is also an opportunity for the girls to share their life experiences with one another as they walk the long distance.

When they arrive at the place where they are to get the reeds, each girl may pick about ten reeds.

On the next day, after breakfast, the girls put on their traditional attire.

The whole celebration takes five days. And the actual dance takes place on the last day.

And the "reed dance," *umhlanga,* is the second most

important ceremony among the Swazi; it's also the mosr colourful. It's for single young women who perform this dance. The "reed dance" is highly significant in its symbolism as a way of paying homeage to the King and to the Queen Mother.

The highest traditional political, economic and ritual powers are shared between a hereditary male ruler, the king, and his mother, the Queen Mother. The dominant institution is aristocracy, and many national officials are drawn from dominant clans, although a balance is somewhat maintained in central and local government between the aristocratic institution and representative democracy.

There are other traditional dances including *sibhaka* which is performed by men in different parts of the country.

The Swazi in South Africa share the same culture with their kith-and-kin in Swaziland.

Men are classified by age groups. The age groups are re-organised every five to seven years. Each age group has its rown responsibilities according to tradition and customs. Traditionally, the Swazi also have a reputation as warriors.

Marriage is conducted in the traditional way but can not take place unless the bridegroom's family has paid dowry, called *lobola*, to the bride's family. Traditional wedding is called *umtsimba*. The Nyakyusa of Tanzania call "wedding" - *ubwegi*. In Swahili, it's called *harusi*.

Among the Swazi, the wedding ceremony is conducted in stages.

Traditionally, the bride and her relatives go to the bridegroom's homestead usually on Friday evening. On Saturday morning, members of the bridal party sit by a nearby river and eat some meat, mainly cow or goat, offered by the brigegroom's family. And in the afternoon, a traditional dance takes place on the premises of the bridegroom's homestead.

On Sunday morning, the bride, with her female relatives, stabs the ground with a spear in the man's cattle kraal, and later she is smeared with red ochre. The smearing is the high point of marriage. No woman can be smeared twice. Then the bride presents gifts to her husband and his relatives.

Polygamy is still practised, although there are those who don't support it for religious and individual reasons. Even Christians practise polygamy except those who believe it's against Biblical teachings and prefer monogamous marriage.

Funerals also have their own rituals. People who attend funerals are considered to be "contaminated" by death. One month after the funeral, the people meet again to wash away the "contamination."

Traditional worship entails invocation of the power of the spirits, although the Swazi have always believed in God as the Supreme Being and the Creator even before the introduction of Christianity.

Therefore, the fundamental difference between the two is not whether or not the Swazi – as well as other Africans who practice traditional religions – believe in the existence of a Supreme Being, who is the one and only, but how they approach Divinity and seek help and guidance from the Creator.

They go through ancestral spirits who intercede with the supernatural on their behalf. The departed ancestors are also given offerings which include sacrifices such as slaughtering cows in order to get some help and guidance from them.

Traditional healers are still common among the Swazi. There are those who use traditional herbs and home-made medicines to provide cures. These are traditional doctors. In Swazi a traditional doctor is called *inyanga*; a term not very much different from *unganga* in Nyakyusa language, and *mganga* in Swahili.

A *sangoma*, usually a woman, is a diviner who

communicates with ancestral spirits and the spirit world to provide solutions to a variety of problems including physical and mental illnesses and social maladies including bad luck and other misfortunes.

And *umtsakatsi* is a witch or a wizard who uses magic to harm or kill people. In Nyakyusa language, a witch or a wizard is called *undosi* or *ndosi*; in Swahili – *mchawi*.

The Swati language is also known as Sewati, Swazi, or isiSwazi. The last term, isiSwazi, is used officially to identify the language. It is also the term used by the Swazi themselves to identify their language.

Swati, or isiSwazi is related to Ndebele, Xhosa and Zulu, and to someone who does not know or understand the language, it is impossible to distinguish it from the other three languages.

Even many people who are familiar with isiSwazi, and with the other three languages, can be easily confused when trying to identify the language because of the strong similarities these language have.

The language has four dialects. And one of the dialects which is spoken in the "deep south" - of South Africa - is highly influenced by Zulu and is not considered to be proper siSwati.

The Swazi are indigenous to South Africa but many of them migrated north and established a new home which later came be known as the country of Swaziland.

And there are strong ties between the people of both countries.

Although Swaziland is predominantly Swazi, Zulus also constitute a significant segment of the country's population. And some of the most prominent South Africans have genealogical ties to Swaziland. They include Miriam Makeba whose mother was a Swazi *sangoma* from Swaziland, and her father a Xhosa indigenous to South Africa.

One of the most well-known and most honoured traditions among the Swazi is the reed dance, an eight-day festival held normally in the last days of August and the first few days of September for all single women. During this highly significant and symbolic cultural event among the Swazi, all unmarried women dance for the Queen Mother and hand over the reeds that have been specially cut for the occasion.

The significance of this ceremony is chastity. It is intended to "protect the women's chastity" and to honour the Queen Mother.

On the last day of the ceremony, the king has some cows slaughtered for a festive occasion during which the women have plenty to eat and even take some of the meat back home with them.

Another major ethnic group in South Africa is the Tsonga.

Historical records by the Portuguese show that when they arrived in the area that came to be known as Mozambique, the Tsonga were already living there in the central and southern parts of that region in the early 1500s.

They were isolated, compared to the way other people lived, and lived peacefully in different settlements here and there without a collective identity. They shared some customs but not a well-organised political structure.

Each Tsonga group occupied its own territory and was named after a a dominant patrilineage.

Their solitary, peaceful life ended when members of other groups fleeing from Shaka's military subjugation in what is now KwaZulu-Natal fled north during the *mfecane* upheaval (1815 - 1840) and entered Tsonga country.

It was an invasion for which the Tsonga were not prepared and they ended up being conquered and dominated by the new comers from the south.

The Nguni group – from the south in KwaZulu – which was the most influential and the strongest after conquering the Tsonga was the Ndwandwe. It was also known as

Shangaan under the leadership of Soshangane.

The Shangaan were a mixture of Nguni - who include the Swazi, Zulu, Ndebele and Xhosa - and Tsonga speakers whom Soshangane conquered and subjugated. The Tsonga speakers included the Ronga, Ndzawu, Shona, Chopi tribes, and their destiny changed after they were conquered by the Zulu led by Soshangane.

Soshangane was a Zulu military leader who established his command over a large Tsonga population in the northern Transvaal in the mid-nineteenth century and continued his conquests farther north. The descendants of some of the conquered populations are known as the Shangaan, or Tsonga-Shangaan.

The first Tsonga-speakers arrived in the former Transvaal in the 1700s, and some Tsonga-Shangaan trace their ancestry to the Zulu warriors who subjugated the armies in the region, while others claim descent from the conquered chiefdoms.

After Soshangane conquered the Tsonga, he made the adoption of Zulu and other Nguni customs mandatory. Also, young Tsonga men were conscripted into the army and taught Zulu military tactics. And he insisted that the Tsonga must learn the Zulu language.

But the Tsonga and the Zulu languages remain separate and are mutually unintelligible in some areas.

The real name in KwaZulu region of the people who invaded and conquered the Tsonga was Ngoni, or Angoni, a tribe whose members migrated as far north as what is now Tanzania. They were related to the Zulu, as they still are today, and live in a number of countries including Mozambique, Malawi, Zambia, and Tanzania.

In fact, the first vice president of Tanganyika – renamed Tanzania in 1964 – after the country won independence from Britain in December 1961 under the leadership of Julius Nyerere was a Ngoni. His name was Rashidi Kawawa. The Ngoni settled in Songea, southern Tanzania, in the 1830s – 1850s, and Kawawa himself came from Songea.

The Ngoni who settled in Mozambique were also known as Angoni or Amashangana, named after their leader Soshangane, and built the Gaza kingdom in the southern part of the country. He named the kingdom after his grandfather and Gaza Province today in Mozambique took its name from that kingdom.

Some of the Tsonga fled Mozambique and settled in what is now the Northern Province in South Africa. Others settled in what later came to be known as Mpumalanga and Limpopo provinces.

In the 18th century, the ancestors of the Tsonga lived in small, independent chiefdoms, sometimes numbering a few thousand people.

They earned a living as hunters in the area which includes what is today known as Kruger National Park. They also lived on fish caught in the rivers in the area where they settled.

Even today, one of the largest groups of the Tsonga still live near Kruger National Park.

The Tsonga-Shangaan homeland, Gazankulu, was carved out of northern Transvaal Province during the 1960s and was granted self-governing status in 1973.

The homeland economy depended largely on gold and on a small manufacturing sector.

Only an estimated 500,000 people - less than half the Tsonga-Shangaan population of South Africa - ever lived there, however. Many others joined the throngs of township residents around urban centers, especially Johannesburg and Pretoria.

Gazankulu later became part of Limpopo Province after the end of white minority rule in April 1994. The Tsonga constitute 23 per cent of the population in the province and are the second-largest group after the Northern Sotho who make up almost 60 per cent.

Traditionally, the Tsonga also had other means of subsistence besides fishing and hunting. They owned goats and chickens, and crop cultivation was also important in their lives. The main crops were maize, cassava, millet, and sorghum. Men cleared the land while women planted and took care of the crops.

Cattle were relatively rare in their economies, probably because their coastal lowland habitat was tsetse-fly infested.

Today, the Tsonga have a mixed economy and live as farmers and livestock owners. Women work on the farms taking of food crops, while some men grow cash crops.

By the 18th century, most Tsonga were organised into several small and independent chiefdoms. And they had a unique system of inheritance under which inheritance was by brothers instead of sons.

It was a defining feature of the Tsonga social system, common in many parts of central Africa but rare among other South African ethnic groups of which the Tsonga were and still are one of them.

Traditionally, their village life was simple. Each Tsonga family had its own homestead composed of a few houses and a kraal, surrounded by the fields and grazing areas.

Even today, their social organisation revolves around the village. They live in scatered villages and each village is occupied by members who have a common patrilineal descent.

Also succession and inheritance are patrilineal. They still practise polygamy and a marriage is sealed only after dowry, usually in the form of cows, has been paid.

The extended family is a form of insurance against disaster and other forms of hardship. And the family's livestock is apportioned among the wives for their support and for eventual inheritance by the children of each household. Widows are supported by males of the dead husband's lineage on his father's side since such obligations are patrilineal.

Traditionally, the Tsonga were ruled by chiefs who exercised considerable authority over their people. And the position of chief was hereditary but subject to approval by a council of elders.

The chief had many responsibilities. They included allocating of land, approving traditional ceremonies involving rituals such as initiation rites, invocation of ancestral guidance and intervention to get rain, and celebrating harvests, among other duties.

He also played the role of mediator in disputes and presided over judicial proceedings.

Traditionally, a Tsonga homestead unit consisted of a large family: a husband, his wife or wives, their children and the families of their married sons.

At first, a married son would stay in his father's homestead but as the son got more wives, he would move out and establish his own homestead.

The sons would usually extend their father's homestead or build next to it. Over time this practice resulted in the formation of clans.

As heads of their families, husbands were treated with great respect by their wives and children. But wives also played important roles, subordinate to their husbands, and were assigned - in extended families – based on their seniority in marriage. The first wife had the highest rank and was accorded respect by junior wives.

Her children also enjoyed higher ranking because of her status as the senior wife; a practice similar to those in different African tribes including the Nyakyusa of Tanzania who also practised polygamy. Authority among wives was also based on seniority among the Nyakyusa, although their children were not necessarily accorded that status, even though such seniority was implied in their case.

The children of the Tsonga played gender roles, just as children in other African tribes do, with the boys being taught by their fathers what to do and playing manly roles such as looking after cattle and goats; while girls were taught at an early age how to be responsible women and followed in the footsteps of their mothers learning how to cook and do other things they were expected to do as women, especially household duties.

Although the family constitutes the basic unit in Tsonga society, the social structure is more complex than that.

The smallest social unit is the 'nuclear family' consisting of a woman with her own hut and cooking area, her husband and their children.

In polygamous families, each mother and children constitute a family unit independent of the others although they all together make up one large family under one leadership: the husband.

And when the sons of an extended family marry, a new homestead called *muti* is established. It is made up of the husband, his wives, their unmarried children and the families of their married sons.

Also there are different social units in the Tsonga traditional society. There are family units as already mentioned; then there are lineages called *nyimba*. The lineages are patrilineal – the father's side – and consist of persons who are lineal descendants and can prove that they are indeed descended from the same ancestors.

The lineages of the people who are related are grouped together to form clans called *xivongo* made up of all persons who have a common ancestor.

The Tsonga social organisation is determined by tribal identity and affiliation. The people of a particular tribe have a chief called *hosi*, and they live in a specific tribal area called *tiko ra hosi*.

The traditional religion of the Tsonga was based on the belief in one God who created the world and everything in it. It was a belief in the Supreme Being. But it was complemented by a belief in the indispensable role of the ancestors as intercessors on behalf of the living.

And although a large number of the Tsonga today are Christian, many them still practise traditional religion which entails constant attention to the propitiation of ancestral spirits. Even among many Tsonga Chrstians, illness and other misfortunes are usually attributed to the breaking of a taboo, to the anger of an ancestor, or to sorcery, just as they are among non-Christians.

Traditional healers also had very important functions in Tsonga society as they still do today. A traditional healer is called *nanga* and provides guidance in consultation with the ancestors. A *nanga* also performs and directs rituals in times of crisis for individuals and for the community.

The term *nanga* is similar to the term the Nyakyusa of Tanzania and Malawi use to describe a person who plays the same role.

A traditional doctor among the Nyakyusa who uses herbs and consults spirits for guidance in providing healing of the sick is called *nganga*. The Swahili term for that is *mganga* which is also used to describe someone who practises modern medicine.

The Nyakyusa term *nganga* also refers to modern doctors as much as it does to a traditional healer. The plural form in Nyakyusa is *baganga*, and in Swahili it's *waganga*.

But the similarities between what the Nyakyusa call *nganga* – or what in Swahili is *mganga* – and what the Tsonga call *nanga* are striking, linguistically, and in terms of social function and the role the traditional healer plays across the spectrum.

The Tsonga believed that man was a physical and spiritual entity but with two separate identities or bodies: the physical and the spiritual, independent of each other, yet inextricably linked and constituting a single entity, with two added attributes: *moya* and *ndzuti*.

The physical body is called *mmiri* in tsonga language, a term similar to *umbili* or *mbili* in Nyakyusa language, and *mwili* in Swahili, all of which mean the same thing: physical body.

Among the Tsonga, what they call *moya* was associated

with the spirit, entered the body at birth and left it at death to join the ancestors. This is similar to a soul in Christian teachings.

Ndzuti reflected human characteristics. Upon death, in the spirit world, it left the body. This meant that the spirit of the dead was imbued with the individual and human characteristics of the person.

Inherent in this concept is not only the belief in life after death but also that the dead retain very strong links with the living. Passing over into the spirit world was an extremely important transition in the lives of the Tsonga as individuals and as a people.

Death was also taken very seriously because of its impact on the family of the departed and on the entire community.

Shortly after death, the members of the family performed a welcoming ceremony to facilitate the passage of the dead person into the spirit world.

The death of a member of the family also caused all the other members in the homestead to become unclean and they all had to go through ritual cleansing ceremonies. These ceremonies were performed at different times of the day over the next few months.

During religious ceremonies the family gathered together at a special area to pay homage to the ancestral spirits. Food and drink was offered to the ancestors to thank them for providing for the people.

Requests were also made to the spirits to intercede in specific situations to solve problems. For more general purposes, the spirits could be approached in a more informal way through prayer.

The existence of both good and evil spirits was a critical component of the Tsonga religious beliefs and traditional way of life.

Good spirits brought rain and caused good things to happen; while evil spirits, controlled by sorcerers, caused great harm to the community. Illness or persistent bad luck usually indicated the presence of evil spirits called *baloyi* but occasional illness was accepted as part and parcel of everyday life.

If a problem persists, whether it's an illness or bad luck, then divine powers must be invoked with the help of traditional healers known as *tin'anga*.

They consult the ancestral spirits by "throwing" the bones which are called *tinholo*, shells or other artefacts and are "able" to determine the cause of the bad luck and suggest ways in which to get rid of the cause.

Traditional healers, also combine magic and the knowledge of medicinal plants called *mirhi* to help and bless the community.

Those who use magic for evil purposes are called *valoyi*, and what they do is called *vuloyi*.

The Nyakyusa of Tanzania have a concept similar to that but the term *balosi* in Nyakyusa language, which is very close to the term *baloyi* in the Tsonga language, refers to people who practise witchcraft to harm people and have spiritual powers - though evil - ordinary people don't have.

Therefore *balosi* in Nyakyusa means "sorcerers." The singular term for that in Nyakyusa is *nlosi*. And "witchcraft" in Nyakyusa is called *bulosi*. And they are similar to *valoyi* and *vuloyi* in Tsonga; so is the term *mlozi* in some African languages, meaning "sorcerer" or "witchdoctor."

However, among the Tsonga, if the illness was serious or the cycle of bad luck persisted, a cure had to be found through divination.

The diviner consulted the ancestral spirits by "throwing" the bones, shells or other artefacts and was thus able to determine the cause of the bad luck and suggest ways in which to get rid of the "cause."

Also in Tsonga traditional religion, some spirits or ancestors are believed to live in certain sacred places where ancient chiefs have been buried. Each clan has several of these burial grounds.

The ancestors are propitiated by prayers and offerings which range from beer to animal sacrifices such as cows. The Sangoma, on behalf of the community, makes offerings in times of trouble or in cases of illness, and on special occasions.

Great care is taken to please the ancestors, as restless ancestors can cause trouble. Children are named after their ancestors to ensure continuity in the family.

According to the Tsonga, there exists a strong relationship between the creation - *ntumbuloko* - and a supernatural power called *Tilo*.

Tilo refers to a vaguely described superior being, who created mankind, but it also refers to the heavens which are the home of this being whose conception by the Tsonga approximates the conception of the Divine among Christians.

The Tsonga also have a great tradition of story telling. Stories are told by the grandmother or an elder woman in the family who is respected as the transmitter of old stories which also serve as a repository of knowledge and wisdom reflecting the life, history, customs and traditions of the people.

They are also known for their traditional music and musical instruments unique to their ethnic group.

The Shangaan–Tsonga people have developed a number of musical instruments which include *fayi*, a small, stubby wooden flute which produces a breathless, raspy, but haunting sound, and is often played by young herd boys; and the *xitende*, a long thin bow tied on each end by a taut leather thong or wire which runs across a gourd.

The *xitende* was often used to alleviate boredom on long journeys. The journeys covered long distances, and the people walked, usually on bare feet as some of them still do today in many parts of the rural areas.

Shangaan–Tsonga male dancers have also traditionally

performed *muchongolo*, a dance which celebrates the role of women in society, war victories, and ritual ceremonies which have always been so important to Tsonga identity as a collective entity.

The Tsonga today constitute a diverse community as an ethnic group or entity and include the Shangaan, the Thonga, and the Tonga – a group not related to the another Tonga group nearby in the north, as well as other smaller groups.

In the mid-1990s, there were about 1.5 million Tsongas in South Africa, and at least 4.5 million in Mozambique and Zimbabwe.

In South Africa, they live mostly in the northeastern part of the country; in Mozambique, in the southern part, and in Zimbabwe in the eastern and southern areas. Also a small number of Shangaans live in Swaziland.

The terms Tsonga and Shangaan are sometimes used interchangeably but Shangaan is quite often used as a synonym for Tsonga.

The Tsonga is a broadly used term encompassing three sub-groups: the Ronga, the Tswa, and the Tsonga also known as Shangaan, a name derived from the Zulu military ruler Soshangane who conquered and ruled the Tsonga. And the three groups are very similar in almost every respect, from language to culture and life style, and merged to create a single ethnic identity.

It is very difficult to determine the population of the Shangaan with accuracy partly because of the confusion that arises from the use of the terms Shangaan and Tsonga. The Tsonga are the larger group among the Shangaan. But it is also a sub-group of the Shangaan, and the term Tsonga is often used to identify the whole group of the Shangaan.

The Tsonga really comprise a number of groups which include the Shangaan, the Thonga, the Tonga as well as a number of smaller groups.

Today, the Shangaan live in areas mainly between the Kruger National Park and the Drakensberg Mountains in

South Africa's Mpumalanga and Northern Provinces.

But what are called Shangaan did not exist as an ethnic group until the Zulu under the leadership of Soshangane entered Tsonga land and imposed his authority on the Tsonga people.

During the *mfecane* and ensuing upheaval of the nineteenth century, most Tsonga chiefdoms moved inland. Some successfully maintained their independence from the Zulu, while others were conquered by Zulu warriors even after they had fled

And their language, Tsonga also known as xiTsonga, is another language which transcends national boundaries. It is spoken in many parts of southern Africa – and not just in South Africa – mostly by the Shangaan.

Besides South Africa, the language is also spoken in Mozambique, Swaziland, Lesotho, and Zimbabwe.

It is spoken by more than 1.6 million people in South Africa's Limpopo, Gauteng and Mpumalanga provinces; 4.5 million in Mozambique; 100,000 in Zimbabwe, and by about 20,000 in Swaziland.

There are also Tsonga speakers in Botswana, Malawi and Zambia but in smaller numbers.

Limpopo Province has the largest number of Shangaans in South Africa. And it borders Mozambique where the Shangaan originated, in Gaza Province, before spreading to other parts of southern Africa.

And the term xiTsonga refers to the Tsonga language spoken in South Africa. It is basically the same language, but there are some differences between the xiTsonga which is spoken in South Africa and the Tsonga that is spoken in Mozambique as well as in other parts of southern Africa.

And although in South Africa the language is spoken mostly in Limpopo Province, as well as in Gauteng and Mpumalanga, it is not uncommon to find the Shangaan in places as far south as KwaZulu-Natal Province speaking their language, xiTsonga.

There are other indigenous Africans in South Africa who are not of Bantu stock. They are the Khoi, or Khoikhoi, and the San. They are the oldest inhabitants in the country.

The Khoi are closely related to the San, so-called Bushmen, and have lived in South Africa, especially in what became the Cape Colony then Cape Province, for at least about 2,000 years.

Archaeological evidence shows that they entered South Africa from what is now the northern part of Botswana.

They avoided the Kalahari desert by going west and then travelling south along the coast all the way down to the Cape. That is where the first white settlers, the Dutch, encountered them centuries later.

They also took another route by travelling southeast. They entered the Highveld and went further down to the southern coast.

The Khoikhoi were named Hottentots by the Dutch settlers.

It is a derogatory term and even gives that impression right away just by the way it sounds.

And it is no more complimentary than the term Bushmen is and which was also first used by Europeans to describe another indigenous group of people, the San, who like the Khoi, still carry the burden of stereotypes about them - even among other Africans - probably more than most African groups with the possible exception of the Pygmies.

Their migration south may have started even farther north beyond what is now Botswana, possibly in what is Tanzania today where there are groups of people, the Hadzapi and the Sandawi, who are related to the Khoi and the San.

The Hadzapi still speak a San language. And the Sandawi language is a Khoisan language related to the Khoi family.

Khoisan languages are indigenous to southern and

eastern Africa which are unique because of their clicks.

When the Khoi arrived in the Cape region, they encountered the San, the original inhabitants, and intermarried with them. Then Bantu groups arrived centuries later.

The Khoi were forced off their land and driven into arid and other inhospitable areas, first by the Bantu, then later by white settlers who also enslaved them.

But in spite of all that, they also intermarried with the Bantu - later with white settlers - and even became an integral part of some black African ethnic groups such as the Xhosa. In fact, Khoi influence among the Xhosa is clearly evident, for example, in terms of vocabulary. The name Xhosa itself is of Khoisan origin.

In fact, both the Xhosa and the Zulu adopted Khoisan clicks which is one of the most distinctive characteristics of their languages. The Zulu language, like Xhosa and other black African languages in South Africa, also has a number of words which are of Khoisan origin.

The Khoi and the San share physical and linguistic characteristics. But they are distinct groups in terms of culture and other aspects. The San are usually identified as hunter-gatherers, while the Khoi are pastoralists as well as farmers.

Genetic evidence also suggests that the San may be the oldest people in the world; they are definitely one of the oldest, together with the Khoi, and a few others.

And although they still exist as a group, the San of South Africa have through the generations been absorbed into the general population of Bantu ethnic groups, as have the Khoi.

All the South African ethnic and racial groups we have looked at here have their own cultures even if many of them are related, as they indeed are. And they all have their own languages they use in their daily lives more than any other language.

But, although South Africa has 11 official languages,

English is the dominant language in national life.

It is also the dominant in the lives of millions of South Africans of all races including those who don't even speak English as the first language.

That is because it is the commercial language. It is also the language of administration and is spoken throughout the country. Even the government itself conducts business in English. It is also the medium of instruction in schools across the country.

Other languages are taught in school. They are also used in different schools where appropriate. But all students learn English. Without English, they can't go far in life in terms of education and employment as well as interaction with other people of different backgrounds and nationalities.

In fact, South Africa is one of the most multicultural countries in the world. In almost all the urban centres of South Africa are people of different ethnic groups and races, from within the country itself, as well as many others including foreigners. They have different backgrounds and cultures, as well as values, and speak different languages.

Yet they are able to live together in this racial and cultural mix, in the rainbow nation, although not without problems as the xenophobic attacks on black African immigrants – by black South Africans through the years since the end of apartheid – tragically demonstrates.

Also the abominable institution of apartheid played a big role in reinforcing racial and cultural differences some of which could have been overcome had racial integration been allowed. But because the policy of apartheid was based on the separation of the races, many cultural differences in South Africa also closely correspond to racial identities. In many cases, each racial group still lives in its own world.

And the most oppressed racial group during apartheid, black Africans, not only live in the rural areas in vast numbers without access to social amenities and other benefits of the modern world; they also remain the most impoverished racial group, a legacy of apartheid which will take many years to overcome, if at all.

But, in spite of all that, an increasing number of blacks are increasingly urbanised and have adopted Western lifestyles – to the detriment of their African identity – and usually speak English and Afrikaans, the two dominant white languages in South Africa, without which upward mobility may be very difficult and even impossible in some cases.

So, in a very tragic way, black Africans sometimes have to abandon their traditional ways of life and become "Europeanised" in order to make progress in a country whose economy is still dominated by whites.

You have to master their languages, English and Afrikaans, and even adopted European lifestyles and values in order to prosper and be socially accepted by those who hold your fate in their hands: whites who control and manipulate the levers of power in the economic arena where apartheid still exists in many fundamental ways.

And although cultural differences between whites and blacks are more pronounced, there are also significant differences among blacks themselves; for example between speakers of the Nguni languages – which are Zulu, Xhosa, Ndebele, Swazi and Tsonga – and those who speak Sotho languages which include Tswana, Sotho (also known as Southern Sotho), Northern Sotho, and Venda. Yet, they are all black black Africans who share many similarities. And many urban blacks speak several black African – or indigenous – languages and mingle easily with members of other groups.

One of the most widely spoken African languages is Zulu which has become the lingua franca in the Johannesburg area, even more so after the end of apartheid which witnessed an influx of black Africans into this metropolis on an unprecedented scale.

But the influx also has had unintended consequences: high crime rates, and xenophobia directed against black African immigrants from other parts of the continent.

The majority of black South Africans are Chrsitians and are mainly members of the Anglican and Roman Catholic churches as well as the black Zion Christian Church. There are other denominations as well, including Methodist, Seventh-Day Adventist and others to which other black Africans belong.

But traditional beliefs are still strong even among those who are Chrsitian. And many of them consult a *sangoma*, a traditional healer who provides divination, counselling, and traditional medicine including herbs which have been used by Africans for centuries to deal with all kinds of maladies including mental illness.

A session with a *sangoma* also involves invocation of ancestral spirits for guidance, protection, and intercession with the divine on behalf of the living.

White South Africans are also predominantly Christian and their values and lifestyles are not very much different from those of other whites in Western Europe, North America and Australia and New Zealand.

The majority of Afrikaners belong to the Dutch Reformed Church which is based on Calvinist teachings. And most whites of British origin are members of the Anglican Church, although some of them belong to the Roman Catholic Church.

Other whites in significant numbers including Portuguese and Greeks. There are also whites of other nationalities who have immigrated to South Africa.

Non-black Christians include Lebanese Arabs and Coloureds.

Culturally, Coloureds are much closer to whites, especially Afrikaners, than they are to black Africans in spite of the discrimination they suffered under the Afrikaner-dominated apartheid regime. But they did not suffer as much as blacks did, and they have the same religious beliefs as Afrikaners do and belong to the Dutch Reformed Church more than any other denomination. And they speak Afrikaans, the language of the Afrikaners.

But there is a small number of Coloureds, known as Cape Malays, especially in the Western Cape Province, who are Muslim.

There are also Jews in significant numbers in South Africa. And they are some of the most successful people in the country; an achievement that is also attributed to their status as whites which has been an asset for other whites in the country, Afrikaners and those of British descent as well as others, enabling them to prosper in a way black people could only dream of.

Another group of South Africans, those of Asian origin – mostly Indian – have been able to preserve their cultural heritage and racial identity from the time their ancestors first arrived in South Africa, mainly as indentured servants brought by the British, and continue to be one of the most homogeneous groups in the country.

They are very clannish – an euphemism for racist on many contexts – like their kith-and-kin in East Africa and elsewhere and hardly intermingle with blacks just as most of them don't in Kenya, Tanzania and other parts of the continent and beyond.

In terms of religious beliefs, they are mostly Hindu or Muslim. They also speak English in a country where this language is quite often a passport to success. Indian languages such as Tamil, Hindi, Telegu and Gujerati are also spoken in their communities.

There are also small communities of Chinese and Japanese in South Africa. But the Chinese community has grown through the decades because of the increasing number of immigrants from China, Hong Kong, and Taiwan.

There are more than 200,000 ethnic Chinese who live in South Africa. And in 2008, the High Court of South

Africa ruled that Chinese South Africans were to be reclassified as black people so that they could benefit from government policies aimed at ending white domination in the private sector.

The Chinese Association of South Africa took the government to court, saying its members had been discriminated against.

The association said their members often failed to qualify for business contracts and job promotions because they were regarded as whites.

The association said Chinese South Africans had faced widespread discrimination during the years of apartheid when they had been classified as people of mixed race, and Chinese activists said they also fought against against apartheid but when apartheid ended, they continued to face discrimination.

The South African parliament passed laws, the Broad-Based Economic Empowerment and the Employment Equity Acts, designed to eradicate the legacy of apartheid which left many black people impoverished.

The new laws give people classed as blacks, Indians and coloureds (mixed-race) employment and other economic benefits over other racial groups.

The Black Economic Employment concept was initiated by the governing ANC to help previously disadvantaged individuals - to start their own businesses or become part of existing companies - thus redressing the country's historic inequalities.

And the ruling by the high court in 2008 provides clarity for corporations in South Africa on the rights of their Chinese staff - who were declared "coloured" under apartheid but are as white today.

The ruling also clearly shows that, in spite of the achievements in many areas of life since the end of white minority rule, the legacy of apartheid persists, and with terrible consequences. For example, a study released in May 2008 showed that white South Africans still earn around 450 per cent more than their black counterparts, 14 years after the end of apartheid.

In other words, apartheid *still exists* in the economic arena, making political power blacks have won virtually meaningless in many fundamental respects in their lives in this rainbow nation.

And increasing migration by a very large number of blacks from the rural areas to the towns and cities across the nation since the end of apartheid has not helped to end economic inequality between blacks and whites. Equality in the economic arena remains an elusive dream and will probably remain so for many years to come.

But urban centres continue to be powerful magnets luring untold numbers of people from the rural areas in pursuit of better life in a country which, potentially, offers more economic opportunities – in its cities and towns – than any other African country.

In fact, South Africa is the most urbanised country on the African continent. But this kind of economic and social transformation also has unintended consequences.

While urbanisation of the society has brought some benefits in terms of modernisation, it has also disrupted the traditional way of life among many urban dwellers, leading to the erosion of traditional values and customs and beliefs which have been central to the well-being of Africans for centuries.

Not all urban dwellers who migrated to towns and cities from the rural areas have lost their traditional values and customs. But many of them have been subjected to the stresses and strains of urban life and modernisation – threatening their identities – they otherwise would not have been subjected to, had they been brought up or continued to live in the rural areas where their roots are, and without which they would not have their true identity as an African people.

Although South Africa is the most urbanised country on the continent, the majority of black Africans still live in the rural areas.

And among whites, it is Afrikaner farmers who live in the rural areas more than any other people of European descent in South Africa including fellow Afrikaners. Besides the farmers, the rest of the Afrikaners and other whites live in towns and cities across the country.

Most of these white farmers are very conservative. And many of them still espouse racist views even after the end of apartheid.

But they have also accepted, grudgingly, the fact that they can not turn back the clock and that history is not on their side regardless of how much they continue to espouse the doctrine of white supremacy.

Theirs is an accommodation to a harsh reality they can not do anything about. They are resigned to fate even if nothing is going to change their beliefs about the races. Many of them will die believing they are better than blacks and other non-whites almost in every conceivable way, as "ordained" by God.

Many people of all races who live in the towns and cities across the nation have an outlook towards life which has been very much shaped by their exposure to the world and other cultures many people in the rural areas are not accustomed to.

They live on the fast lane, and in the limelight. And they are "sophisticated" because of their way of life and knowledge of the world. It is a way of life, and an attitude, that fosters materialistic values.

They are not necessarily less spiritualistic than the country dwellers; nor are they necessarily arrogant because they live in the towns and cities. But many of them are.

And those who feel and think that way also tend to think that they are better than the people who live in the villages and in other parts of the rural areas.

This attitude is also reinforced by a belief, a common belief, among millions of people in the rural areas – where they are trapped in poverty – that life in the cities is better, glamorous, with magnificent bounties one can only dream of in the villages.

There is also competition even among the urban dwellers of different cities and towns.

Many of those who live in Johannesburg, the largest and most developed city in South Africa and on the entire continent, may feel that they are on top of the rest – if not the world; and that the people in other cities are not in their league.

That may indeed be the case, from their perspective. But others may feel the same way. It's not uncommon to find Capetonians who feel that life in Cape Town is better than life in Johannesburg and anywhere else in the country.

In fact, many Capetonians are said to have a "superior attitude" which some people may see as arrogance.

But they are no exception.

Such attitudes are an integral part of national life, a cultural phenomenon one should expect in a multicultural society such as South Africa where the people, even when they co-exist, are bound to differ and clash because they are different for different reasons even if they are all members of the same society and constitute one nation.

It's always a major challenge to unite people under one leadership and have them share and articulate a common vision when they have such different backgrounds, customs and beliefs as they do in South Africa.

It is an exercise in social engineering few countries have successfully completed even under committed leadership. And South Africa still has a long way to go.

But South Africa also is a nation which is a union in diversity, giving full expression to many separate identities while at the same time fostering a single identity that transcends the differences within.

South Africa is a land of contrasts, not only in its landscape but also in its people; a phenomenon not peculiar to this rainbow nation.

However, some of these differences have also bred intolerance in a country that has been hailed, because of its triumph over apartheid without retribution, as a model for tolerance.

Part IV:

Black African Immigrants

BLACK Africans mostly from the countries of Southern Africa have migrated to South Africa through decades to work in the mines and other sectors of the economy.

During white minority rule, especially in the 1950s, the apartheid regime even provided free transport for Africans from neighbouring countries who wanted to work in the mines.

They came mostly from Basutoland (now Lesotho), Bechuanaland (Botswana), Nyasaland (Malawi), Southern Rhodesia (Zimbabwe), Northern Rhodesia (Zambia), and Tanganyika (now Tanzania) when the countries were still under colonial rule. All these countries were once ruled by Britain.

But the recruitment of African labour did not continue in all the countries after they won independence. Tanganyika under the leadership of President Julius Nyerere stopped its citizens from going to South Africa even to visit let alone work because of that country's racist policies of apartheid.

But there were many Tanganyikans already working in the mines in South Africa and many of them, if not the majority, stayed in South Africa even after their country won independence from Britain in December 1961. And they are still there today, together with their children and grandchildren Others, as Tanzanians, migrated to South Africa after apartheid ended in 1994.

One Tanzanian writer, Godfrey Mwakikagile, recalls how his fellow countrymen left Tanganyika (as the country was then known before uniting with Zanzibar in 1964 to form Tanzania) to work in the mines in South Africa, and even in Northern Rhodesia and the Belgian Congo in the 1950s and before then.

Members of his tribe, the Nyakyusa, constituted one of the largest ethnic groups of migrant workers from Tanganyika who went to work in the mines in South Africa in the 1950s.

And in an ironic twist, some of the migrant workers from Tanganyika who were recruited as labourers to work in the South African mines had originally migrated from South Africa to Tanganyika. They were the Ngoni. As Godfrey Mwakikagile states in his book, *Life in Tanganyika in The Fifties*:

"The fifties were without question some of the most important years of my life. They were my formative years as much as the sixties were. And I remember listening to many inspiring stories which helped to enlarge my mental horizon at such an early age. And they have remained a source of inspiration throughout my life. My father was one of the people who liked to tell stories about hard work and success in life and played a critical role in shaping my personality when I was growing up.

I also remember hearing stories of valour about the Nyakyusa during my time and in the past including their successful campaigns against the Ngoni in the 1830s, '40s and '50s when the Ngoni tried to invade and penetrate

Nyakyusaland. The Nyakyusa also successfully repelled the Sangu who invaded our district in the 1870s and 1880s from neighbouring Usangu in Mbeya District. Like the Nyakyusa, the Sangu had a quite a reputation as fierce fighters. But they were no match for the Nyakyusa who stopped their incursions into Nyakyusaland.

The few white missionaries who settled in Rungwe District also tried to intervene and act as mediators in the conflicts not only between the Nyakyusa and the Sangu but also between the Nyakyusa and the Safwa, then the largest ethnic group in Mbeya District until they were later outnumbered by the Nyakyusa. They also played a mediating role in other conflicts including intra-tribal (or intra-ethnic) disputes but not always successfully.

But, besides the Nyakyusa, it was the Ngoni whom I remember the most for their reputation as fighters mainly because I interacted with them in the sixties. Their legendary reputation as fighters sent a chill down the spine and many of their neighbours were afraid of them, except a few like the Nyakyusa, and the Hehe who, under their leader Chief Mkwawa, once defeated the Germans.

Originally from Natal Province in South Africa, the Ngoni settled in Songea District in southern Tanganyika, as well as in Sumbawanga in the western part of the country where they came to be known as the Fipa, which is their ethnic name and identity even today. They had a reputation as fierce fighters even in South Africa itself before they left during the *imfecane* in the 1820s and '30s headed north, finally settling in what is now Malawi, Mozambique and Tanzania. Some of them even went to Congo after going through Tanganyika.

I went to Songea Secondary School which was a boarding school in Songea District, the home district of the Ngoni, in southern Tanzania and talked to many Ngonis including some who were old enough to be my parents when I was in my teens back then in the sixties. Almost without exception, they all recalled the stories they were told by their elders when they were growing up on how the Nyakyusa and the Ngoni fought when the Ngoni tried to invade and conquer Nyakyusaland, to no avail.

They told me that the Nyakyusa *ni watani wetu*, a Swahili expression meaning they are our friends and we tell jokes about each other. Many of those "jokes" have to do with how hard the Nyakyusa fought to repel the Ngoni invaders after the Ngoni failed to steal Nyakyusa cows and women!

Some of the Ngoni also went to work in the mines in South Africa - where they originally came from - but not in significant numbers as the Nyakyusa and other people from the Southern Highlands did, especially from Rungwe and Mbeya Districts in a region bordering what was then Northern Rhodesia, now Zambia.

Northern Rhodesia itself attracted many mine workers from my region and many of them settled in that country. Even today, you will find many Nyakyusas who settled in Kitwe and other parts of the Copperbelt many years ago after they went to work there in the mines. For example, in 1954 the Nyakyusa in Kitwe formed an organisation to preserve, protect and promote their interests as a collective entity.

The Lozi, members of another ethnic group from Baraotseland or Barotse Province and one of the largest in Zambia, also formed their own organisation around the same time, as did others and some even before then including the Ngoni. And they were all cited as examples of ethnic solidarity among the mine workers in Kitwe and other parts of the Copperbelt in Northern Rhodesia. The Nyakyusa presence in what is now Zambia is still strong even today.

In fact, one of my mother's first cousins who was older than my mother emigrated from Tanganyika to Northern Rhodesia as a young man in the early 1940s. He was the son of my mother's uncle Asegelile Mwankemwa who was the pastor of our church, Kyimbila Moravian Church at

Kyimbila in Rungwe District. He also lived in South Africa for a number of years before returning to Northern Rhodesia where he eventually became a high government official after the country won independence as Zambia.

He returned to Tanzania in the 1990s to spend his last days in the land of his birth. Tragically, he had forgotten Kinyakyusa and did not know Kiswahili after so many years of absence from Tanganyika, later Tanzania, and could communicate only in English and Bemba, one of the major languages in Zambia. All his children were also born and brought up in Northern Rhodesia.

And he was just one of the many people from my district who migrated to Northern Rhodesia and even some of them to South Africa. Jobs in the mines in both countries was the biggest attraction, encouraging many Tanganyikans to go there in those days.

The town of Mbeya was their main departure point heading south and was the largest town in the region. It was also the capital of the Southern Highlands Province when I was growing up.

The people who had been recruited to work in the mines in South Africa boarded planes called WENELA. I remember that name very well because I heard it all the time when I was growing up in the fifties. The people would say so-and-so has gone to Wenela, meaning to work in the mines in South Africa. The term became an integral part of our vocabulary in the 1950s, probably as much as it was even before then among the Nyakyusa and others.

The name WENELA was an acronym for the Witwatersrand Native Labour Association which was responsible for the recruitment of cheap labour among Africans in neighbouring countries including Tanganyika to work in the mines in South Africa. They were sometimes recruited to work in other sectors of the economy but primarily in the mines.

Many of the people who were recruited in Tanganyika were flown down there unlike, for example, those from

Basutoland (now Lesotho) or Bechuanaland (now Botswana) who, because of their proximity to South Africa, were transported by buses.

But many people from Tanganyika were also transported by road from Mbeya in the Southern Highlands to Broken Hill in Northern Rhodesia. And from there they were taken to Mungu in Barotseland, the western province of Northern Rhodesia, and then flown to Francistown in Bechuanaland; and finally transported by railway to Johannesburg.

Working in the mines was hard labour, with little pay. But it was still something for people who virtually had nothing in terms of money. That's why they were drawn down there.

I remember my cousin Daudi worked for three years in the mines in Johannesburg. But when he came back to Tanganyika, he hardly had anything besides a wooden box he used as a "suitcase" - and which was the only popular and common "suitcase" among many Africans in those days - and may be a couple of shirts, two pairs of trousers, and a simple pair of shoes he wore when he returned home. In fact, he came straight to our village, from Johannesburg, to live with us.

My father was also his father, and the only one had, since his own biological father migrated to South Africa. His father left behind two children, Daudi himself, and his only sister, Esther, who was also younger than Daudi. Tragically, she died only a few years after Daudi returned from South Africa.

He went to South Africa to earn some money, yet returned hardly with any. It was hard life not only for him but for most Africans who went to work in the mines and even for those who remained in the villages.

In general the people were not starving in Tanganyika in the fifties. There was plenty of food especially in fertile regions such as the Southern Highlands where I come from. And my home district of Rungwe is one of the most fertile in the entire East Africa and on the whole continent. Almost anything, any kind of food, grows there: from bananas to sweet potatoes, groundnuts to beans, and all kinds of fruits and vegetables, besides cash crops such as coffee and tea, and much more.

But the people were poor in terms of financial resources. They had very little money. And that is why some of them went all the way to South Africa and to neighbouring Northern Rhodesia to work in the mines.

Some of them also ended up in Katanga Province, in the Congo, which is about 300 miles west from my home region of Mbeya. With all its minerals as the treasure trove of Congo, Katanga Province was another prime destination for job seekers from neighbouring countries who were looking for jobs in the mines.

The Nyakyusa from my home district were some of the people who ended up there. For example, I vividly remember a photograph of a Nyakyusa family published in the *Daily News*, Dar es Salaam, when I worked there as a news reporter in the early seventies.

They had lived in Congo for about 40 years but were expelled from the country and forced to return to Tanzania in what seemed to be a xenophobic campaign fuelled by anti-foreign sentiments in spite of the fact that members of this family, as well as many others, had lived in Congo for decades and their children were born and brought up there.

Therefore there was quite a contrast in terms of living standards between Africans and Europeans as well as between Africans and Asians; also between Africans and Arabs. Africans were the poorest. But there was no hostility, at least not overt, on the part of Africans towards whites and others in spite of such disparity in living standards; not to the extent that the social order was threatened in a way that could have led to chaos in the country." (Godfrey Mwakikagile, *Life in Tanganyika in The Fifties*, Second Edition, Continental Press, 2007, pp. 110 – 114).

Tanzania is one of the few African countries which have been spared the agony of violent ethnic and racial convulsions on this turbulent continent. For decades, Tanzania also has been a haven for the largest number of refugees on the continent. In fact, it has had one of the largest refugee populations in the entire world since the 1950s.

Some of the refugees came from South Africa during the apartheid era and they lived without being harassed, intimidated or attacked by their hosts, Tanzanians. They were welcomed with open arms. And many of them still live in Tanzania.

Ironically, some of the biggest victims of the xenophobic violence in South Africa since the end of apartheid have been Tanzanians whose country sacrificed some much to help black people in South Africa win their freedom.

Some of the Tanzanians, like many other Africans from different parts of Africa, were married to South Africans. Therefore for those who had some children, their children were South African by birth. Citizenship was their birth right. Yet many black South Africans did not accept them because one of their parents was a foreigner, although just from another African country and was therefore a fellow African.

Black South Africans also accused black African immigrants of stealing their women, on top of stealing their jobs and even their houses. And many of them were accused of bribing local officials to get the houses even though a significant number of them bought the houses and did not take any short cuts to get them.

It didn't matter that the people they were attacking also had rights as fellow human beings. They had human rights but according to their attackers they had none.

It also didn't matter that the people they were attacking came from the countries which not only sacrificed so much in terms of material and financial support to help black South Africans who fled to those countries during apartheid; these countries, Tanzania and others, also lost hundreds and even thousands of people during the liberation struggle when the apartheid regime inflicted heavy punishment, and heavy casualties, on them for supporting blacks in South Africa in their quest for freedom.

And it didn't matter that many of them also had the legal right to live in South Africa. And for those who did not have that, they were, at the very least, entitled to compassion from their hosts as fellow human beings, as fellow Africans, and as compatriots in the liberation struggle during apartheid.

Nicole Johnson, a reporter of one of South Africa's leading newspapers, the *Mail&Guardian*, visited one such family – the head of the family was a Tanzanian – and had this to say in her report published in the 24 May 2008 edition of the *Mail&Guardian*, entitled, "'Tell Them We're From Here'":

Sunday

"The battles raging on the streets of Jeppestown on Sunday (18 May 2008) couldn't crack my journalistic composure, but Mohamed made me cry. He's seven years old, beautiful and sparky and he's been driven from his home because he has a Tanzanian father.

Mohamed Fall was born in Johannesburg General Hospital, his mother is South African and he is in grade 2 at John Mitchell Primary in Jeppestown.

Until Saturday night they lived in the Radium Hotel in Jeppestown.

'At night they came, they were hitting the gate. They made a big noise and they chased us,' Mohamed says. He watched as they destroyed the hotel he has called home for most of his life. 'They broke the bar and they took the beers and the coins and the money.'

And he watched as they tried to assault his mother, Tracy Aspelling, accusing her of being a Zimbabwean. She survived because she is from Port Elizabeth and managed to convince them of this.

That wasn't enough to save their home or belongings, though. 'We just left our stuff and ran,' says Aspelling. As they ran, they saw the neighbourhood being destroyed by looters: 'They have sticks and they hit the shops and steal clothes,' Mohamed told me. 'I think they're sick.

'We don't know where to sleep so we came here,' he says. Tracy is adamant that she will not be driven out of the country. 'I was born here. I am not going anywhere.' Mohamed is less sure: 'It will happen again,' he says matter of factly. 'I don't feel nice -- I feel bad.'

As he sits in the courtyard of the police station on Sunday afternoon, in his neatly pressed coffee-coloured shirt and shorts, he seems remarkably composed. Both he and his mother seem determined to continue as normal. She plans to go to work the next day. 'I need to go to school tomorrow,' Mohamed tells me resolutely. Then his face falls as he remembers afresh: 'They broke our house and took my uniform.'

Monday

Mohamed doesn't go to school on Monday. The number of refugees in the police station has doubled overnight.

New, bloodied victims continue to stream in and the police are reluctant to let anyone out. His mother doesn't have the money for school transport anyway -- her purse was one of the first things the mob stole. 'My mom said I mustn't go to school.'

Mohamed feels reassured because he is not the only one missing school -- lots more children have turned up, including twins Annie and Rose Bofonge (8), who are in his grade 2 class at John Mitchell. They sit under a marquee erected for mothers with children, playing clapping games and giggling. 'We only got oranges and sweets yesterday. I was hungry at night. It was cold at night and I had only a small blanket.'

At lunchtime the food supply in the makeshift refugee camp is erratic. 'I just got food now, two slices of bread, Mohamed says. It's the first thing he's eaten all day.

His mother has somehow managed to get out of the station and go to her job at a shop in the area. She is terrified she will be replaced if she doesn't show up and also of being unemployed and homeless. Having an income is her only chance of rebuilding her family when this madness has passed.

As I leave, Mohamed extracts two promises from me -- that I will come see him the next day and that I spread the word: 'Tell them we are not the foreigners. We are the South Africans.'

Tuesday

By Tuesday evening the children are all a lot more subdued. Days of sleeping outdoors in Jo'burg's winter, of overcrowding, inadequate food and nowhere to wash are taking their toll.

Mohamed's clothes are dirty and crumpled and he appears to have lost a shoe.

A local resident has brought him a jersey to put over his short-sleeved shirt and shorts. Women sing and dance, clapping and stamping among the towering piles of bags and belongings, trying to keep their spirits up and to keep warm.

Mohamed's mother sits on a bundle of someone's possessions, her arm around her child, staring dully at what has become her world in the past few days. They don't feel much like talking."

Another victim whose his plight was also brought to national attention in South Africa and elsewhere after what happened to him was reported in the same paper, the *Mail&Guardian*, was Percy Zvumoya, a journalist from Zimbabwe, whose country also sacrificed so much to help black South Africans win their freedom.

And like thousands of black African immigrants who had lived in peace and harmony with their neighbours, many of them for years, Percy Zvumoya also found out that his neighbours turned against him.

Obviously, the relative peace and harmony the black African immigrants enjoyed living with their black South African neighbours was more apparent than real.

Little did they know that there was latent hostility among their black South African neighbours which would one day bubble to the surface and explode.

Percy Zvumoya's story, written by himself, was published in the 24 May 2008 edition of the *Mail&Guardian* under the headline, "'You Can't Imagine The Pain'":

"I was about to retire for the night last Thursday (22 May) when a group of people came in and said: "Get out and give us the keys to this place". I negotiated with them and they allowed me take a few things like clothing.

I fled from my house into the township. I came back later because I had nowhere else to go. I was really scared, I couldn't get back into the house and hid on the roof from where I made a call to the police.

They advised me to leave. They told me they couldn't do much because they were stretched. In the morning I went to my employer's house and stayed there.

When I went back to my house the following day [Friday] they had taken my DVD player, my television and my bed. I could only retrieve the fridge which they had not carried away. I left the fridge with friends in the township.

I came to South Africa from Zimbabwe when I was

about 18, that was in 1989. But I am now a citizen, I got my ID book last year. My wife still lives in Zimbabwe with our three children. I am here to work and to support my family. I don't know what I have done. I have been living well with my neighbours.

But when this broke out even my neighbours, people I have lived with for 13 years, were shouting: "He should go. He is a Kalanga" [Kalanga is a tribe found in southern Zimbabwe and the north of Botswana]. These are people I have lived with and they sold me out because they were jealous of the little that I had gathered.

Even if things return to normal I don't think I can live with these people again. I don't think I can go back.

I built that house myself. Before it was a tin shack and rats were getting in. I thought I should build a proper house, I built it slowly, buying a brick at a time. And now people just came and order me out. It's painful.

I didn't borrow from anyone to buy all these things. I earned them with the sweat of my brow. But I guess I should forget about these things, there is nothing I can do.

I can't understand the rationale of all this. I am a citizen of this state. I was chased from my own home. I don't know what I am supposed to do or where I am supposed to go.

I guess I will work again. I still have the strength. I can't go back to Alex. Maybe I should go back to the country of my birth. But it's bad there too.

I was planning on my kids coming here, but not when it's like this. There is so much suffering in Zim-babwe, but it would be better for them to stay there.

You can't imagine the pain I went through after my ordeal. I cried the whole night. Have you ever cried the whole night? I thought I was going to get hypertension or something.

I talked to some people who were displaced like me. Some suggested we should douse the whole street with petrol and burn the whole neighbourhood. I firmly said no.

We can't do that. We shouldn't [take] revenge. God is for us all. He is the one who should judge. You see all these kids? Can you imagine them dead? I said no. We would hurt many innocent people who have nothing to do with this thuggery.

What I can't understand about this is how would foreign-based South Africans react if other countries in the world chased them away? That would be barbaric.

Do you remember that during apartheid South Africans were living in Zimbabwe, Zambia, Tanzania, Britain and many other places? I wonder how this violence will end but I know many people will die.

Did you see the picture of the man who was burnt to death? How can women watch someone burn to death and laugh?

Why did they give me citizenship? So that mobs burn me while some people laugh?"

Many South Africans, in condemning the violence, reminded their fellow countrymen of the sympathy and kindness South Africans were accorded by other African countries during apartheid. As the secretary-general of the ruling African National Congress (ANC), Gwede Mantashe, stated on Friday, 23 May 2008, one day after the violence against black African foreigners erupted in Cape Town and 12 days after the attacks first started farther north in the township of Alexandra near Johannesburg:

"Many of us, including myself, will think of the kindness we received in the poorest communities of Angola, Mozambique, Zimbabwe, Zambia, Tanzania, Nigeria and many other African states.

We will recall that our neighbours were collectively punished by the apartheid regime for harbouring the cadres of the ANC.

We will remember that our children were given spaces

in overcrowded schools in remote rural villages, and when we were injured and ill, the hospitals of many African countries nursed us back to health."

He was quoted by the *Mail&Guardian* in its main news report, "'Deliberate Effort' Behind Attacks," Friday, 22 May 2008.

As an expression of solidarity with the suffering black South Africans, Tanganyika was the first country in the region to sever links with the apartheid regime. The ties between the two countries existed during colonial rule. And she refused to establish diplomatic and commercial ties with the apartheid regime because of her uncompromising opposition to the country's racist policies which denied blacks and other non-whites equality.

But although Tanganyika did not allow her citizens to go to South Africa during the apartheid era after the country won independence in 1961, she did not have much company in the region in that respect.

People from the other countries in the region never stopped going to South Africa to work in the mines after their countries won independence. And the migratory trend has continued through the years, with even much larger numbers of them going to South Africa after the end of apartheid.

The end of apartheid ushered the dawn of new era not only for South Africa but for the entire continent. One of the most significant developments was the increase in immigration of a large number of people into South Africa from the other countries on the continent, mostly those in sub-Saharan Africa.

The immigrants, legal and illegal, were drawn to South Africa by employment opportunities and better living conditions in the most developed country on the continent. But they found out that they were not always welcome in the new South Africa. As Suzanne Daley, reporting from South Africa, stated in her report in *The New York Times*,

19 October 1998, entitled, "New South Africa Shuts the Door on Its Neighbors":

"The anonymous caller to the police claimed that there were many illegal immigrants working at the Galaxy clothing shop downtown.

But among the cardboard boxes of cheap blue jeans and polyester shirts, the police found only one likely suspect -- a neatly dressed young salesman with the sharp features, dark skin and wavy hair of a northern African. When he could not produce identity papers, the immigration officers quietly escorted him to their prison bus.

On the street, pedestrians quickly recognized the arrest for what it was and began to applaud. Then a taxi driver started chanting, pumping his fist out the window of his van: "Go home!" he shouted. "Go home!" Soon it was a full-fledged chorus, loud enough to drown out the screech of the rusting bus door closing behind the prisoner -- the ninth to be collected on a recent morning.

Drawn to President Nelson Mandela's new democracy and an economy that dwarfs all others on this continent, illegal immigrants from all over Africa, many of them destitute, are pouring into this country in ever greater numbers, experts say. But they are hardly finding a welcome mat.

The economy here is failing to grow as fast as predicted, and majority rule has failed to produce enough housing, health clinics and good schools. So South Africans are growing increasingly resentful of the new arrivals, seeing them as thieves of scarce resources.

Many of the apartheid-era efforts to keep the country's borders secure have been relaxed. But current hardship and past isolation have left the country ill prepared to deal with this growing problem. Surveys suggest that anti-foreigner attitudes, particularly against blacks, are deep-seated and widespread among all races. And violence against immigrants is growing.

Last month, an angry mob killed three foreigners on a commuter train outside Pretoria after accusing them of stealing jobs from South Africans. Two of the victims, both from Senegal, were electrocuted when they climbed onto the roof to escape being lashed with cattle whips. The third, a Mozambican, was thrown out the window and killed by an oncoming train.

The incident was hardly the only recent brutality against foreigners. In Cape Town, at least 10 died in the last year in assaults that the police believe were related to anti-immigrant sentiments.

In downtown Johannesburg, local hawkers have repeatedly demonstrated against foreign ones, and each time some foreigners are beaten and robbed.

In Alexandra township, inside the wealthy suburb of Sandton, armed gangs have assaulted immigrants and marched them to the police station to "clean" the area of foreigners. And in the eastern province of Mpumalanga last summer, a gang calling itself the Unemployed Group ambushed and burned at least six trucks as part of what it called a "torch campaign" to force companies to give jobs to locals.

Concerned about the pattern, the Human Rights Commission sponsored a symposium this week to get business and community leaders thinking about the issue.

"Even with the Pretoria train attack, the reaction was very muted," said Jody Kollapen, a commission member who describes animosity toward immigrants as having risen sharply in the last five years. "There was very little public outcry. That silence is of great concern to us."

Recent surveys show that South Africans are among the world's most xenophobic people. Twenty-five percent want a ban on immigrants, according to one survey, taken last year by the Institute for Democracy in South Africa, a nonprofit research group based in Cape Town. Just two years earlier that number was 16 percent.

Foreign Blacks Face Greater Antagonism

The same survey found that about 80 percent of those polled said they had little or no contact with foreigners. Moreover, both black and white South Africans prefer white immigrants, viewing newcomers from Europe and North America more favorably than they do Africans.

There is a debate about what may be behind such attitudes. One of the authors of the institute's survey, Dr. Robert Mattes, says he thinks the intolerance may have grown out of a society that for decades carefully separated races and encouraged the denigration of blacks.

"There is a very paternalistic and antagonistic view of blacks north of the border," Dr. Mattes said. "They are seen as wetbacks, yokels, rural folks. They are definitely not like us."

But others argue that the xenophobia may simply be a passing mood the country is feeling as it forges a new national identity and copes with difficult economic times.

White-ruled South Africa strictly controlled the number of immigrants allowed in as cheap labor. Borders were patrolled and mined. An electric fence -- its voltage set to kill -- stood between South Africa and Mozambique.

But such restrictions have eased under the Government of the African National Congress, which in many ways owes its very existence to its neighbors. Many exiled A.N.C. leaders sat out the apartheid era or plotted their guerrilla attacks in neighboring countries that risked the vengeance of an often-brutal apartheid Government.

Estimates of the illegal immigrant population in South Africa now vary widely, from two million to eight million, and are regarded by most experts as hardly more than guesses.

What is clear, however, is that South Africa -- which according to the latest census figures has a population of 37 million -- has been deporting more and more immigrants each year, nearly 200,000 in 1997.

For much of the continent, South Africa is the pot of gold at its end, and each new war or famine sets off a wave of new arrivals desperate to work on farms or building sites for a pittance, or even for a daily bowl of porridge. Many end up at the lowest rungs of the economy and live clustered together, creating their own neighborhoods.

The biggest influx comes from Mozambique, which has been ravaged by nearly 20 years of civil war. The Kruger Park forms most of the border between the two countries, and every year an unknown number of the thousands of Mozambicans trying to cross are eaten by lions -- which then must be hunted down and shot because they have developed a taste for human flesh.

Last year during an autopsy of one lion, a purse with $1.50 in Mozambican currency was found in its stomach.

Desperate Measures to Cross the Border

South of the park, about 40 miles of electric fence still stands. The voltage is now set to give only a strong shock. Soldiers monitor computers that sound alarms whenever it is breached, and they take up the chase.

Many immigrants slip through by running into the sugar cane fields, emerging on roads where they catch minivan taxis to carry them away quickly.

Last year the Army Group 33, which patrols near Komatipoort, arrested about 22,000 border-jumpers. It keeps them overnight in a large holding cell on its base, gives them breakfast and takes them back to Mozambique. But officials say most simply try again the next day, which makes it difficult to keep up the soldiers' morale.

"I think when you catch the same guy three times in four days, it can get pretty frustrating," said Capt. Gustav Brink, who is in charge of one of the units that patrol the fence.

One day earlier this year, Marcos Toal, 17, who had been caught within seconds of sliding under the fence, was in the "cage" waiting to be taken back across the border.

This, his first attempt, had ended badly. He had started with a change of clothes and $30 -- enough, he hoped, to reach "Egoli," the city of gold, also known as Johannesburg. But he had been robbed on the Mozambican side by men demanding payment as guides through the fence.

Though he was clearly frightened that he would be beaten, he was sure he would be trying again. South Africa is his only hope of making enough money to marry and get started in life.

"People speak of South Africa and they say it is a place where you can get work and make a living without having to turn to crime," he said.

Since 1994 South Africa has been drafting a policy to admit immigrants who have sought-after skills. Officials also realize that the country's neighbors need investment, too, to keep their citizens at home.

But none of this stops politicians from routinely using foreigners as scapegoats for everything from rising crime to unemployment to AIDS, and the Government has taken no step to address the popular hostility.

Rights Group Finds Abuse of Immigrants

In a report released this year, Human Rights Watch condemned South Africa's xenophobia and documented abuses of immigrants, including beatings, extortion by the police and arbitrary arrests.

Both legal immigrants and South Africans are the targets of these abuses, especially if they have very dark skins or inoculation marks on their forearms. Most local people have these marks on their upper arms.

Foreigners, too, say they feel growing xenophobia, according to a new report by the Center for Policy Studies, a research group based in Johannesburg.

Ade Ogunrinade, a Nigerian who is the deputy vice chancellor of the Witwatersrand University here, was quoted in a recent newspaper article as saying that his wife had had difficulty finding a job and that they had both felt hostility because they are foreigners.

"In West Africa we have a tradition of warmth to foreigners," Mr. Ogunrinade said. "I find it disconcerting that the same warmth is not experienced here."

Peter Takirambudde, executive director of the Africa Division of Human Rights Watch, took South Africans to task for a lack of compassion.

"During the apartheid era," he said, "many African countries opened their doors to South African migrants, exiles and refugees and paid a heavy economic price for their opposition to apartheid. Now that the tables are turned, it is shameful to see how hostile South Africans have become."

Authorities refused requests to visit Lindela, the holding installation for immigrants in the Johannesburg area. But when the young downtown salesman was taken there, a brief glimpse was possible. An official interviewing new arrivals could be seen repeatedly striking a young man, apparently unsatisfied with his answers.

Police officers working for the Johannesburg police units tracking down illegal immigrants said arrests can be almost laughably easy. Sometimes the police simply send a van to a certain corner pretending to be a taxi, and immigrants climb in.

Some would-be immigrants have intricate schemes for getting false papers, including paying tribal chiefs in rural areas to certify false parents for them. But many cannot afford papers, and so barely eke out an existence because they are taken advantage of by unscrupulous employers and landlords.

"Everybody looks at South Africa and sees it as the land of milk and honey,' said Superintendent Montiers Stein, who runs one of the units. 'But it doesn't turn out that way for a lot of them.'"

So, hostility towards black African immigrants, by black South Africans, is nothing new. Contempt for them among many black South Africans who think they are better than other black Africans - because they are indigenous to the most developed country on the continent - is nothing new either.

Yet – and I'll be brutally frank about it – black South Africans *can not* legitimately claim, on the same level with whites, to have contributed to the technological progress of South Africa which enabled it to become the most advanced country on the continent. So they're claiming credit for something they did *not* do. And the reason is simple.

Black South Africans did not get the opportunity to get the kind of education whites did which would have enabled them to contribute to th country's technological progress.

Throughout the nation's history, black South Africans have contributed manual labour, *not* scientific knowledge, towards national development. There have been a number of educated black South Africans in many scientific fields, but not many to have had a significant impact on the country's technological progress.

It's not that they're not intelligent – they are, and well-endowed in terms of mental faculties, just like other Africans as well as other human beings. But they have never had the skills and the kind of education whites have had to develop the country as an industrial and technologically advanced society.

It was *white* South Africans, *not black* South Africans, who developed South Africa as a technologically advanced society. If *all* highly skilled whites pull out of South Africa today, the country would collapse overnight! Even sensible black South Africans acknowledge that their country will be in trouble if that happens.

In fact, black people in many African countries are far more educated than black South Africans are. And that includes many black African immigrants in South Africa, the very same people black South Africans despise so much.

Take Nigeria as an example. The number of highly educated people Nigeria has is something black South Africans can only dream of. And many other African countries such as Zimbabwe, Ghana, Uganda, Kenya, Tanzania and Ethiopia have far more educated people than *black* South Africans have.

Yet, these are the very same people many black South Africans despise as *makwerekwere*.

Many South African employers hire blacks from other African countries, *not* because they are not black South Africans; they hire them because they are more qualified for the jobs than black South Africans are.

Yet the contempt for black Africans from other countries, among many black South Africans, is an enduring phenomenon, even though it is the kind of contempt that comes from a false sense of pride.

Black South Africans have the right to be proud of their country. But they have *no right – none whatsoever –* to claim as theirs the contribution made by educated white South Africans in the development of South Africa as a technologically advanced society, at least on the African continent, even if in many respects (not all) it's just another Third World country in a global context.

Black South Africans should *not* claim credit for the technological development of South Africa in the scientific arena. They have contribute little in the scientific realm.

Without the professional and technological skills of white South Africans, responsible for the nation's industrial and technological progress black South Africans are so much proud of, South Africa would be just another African country, very underdeveloped, and everything else that goes with it: no infrastructure, no institutional capacity, and much more.

That is the truth, the bitter truth, black South Africans

who despise other black Africans *need* to be told when they call other Africans *makwerkwere*.

Not all black South Africans feel that way but those who do need to be told the truth.

It is a bitter pill to swallow, but they need to swallow it, together with their false sense of pride, thinking that they are the ones who developed South Africa as the most technologically advanced society on the African continent in sharp contrast with the other countries to the north. They're deluding themselves!

And it is this delusional thinking which also explains why many of them call black Africans from other African countries *makwerekwere*.

The term *makwerekwere* or *amakwerekwere* says it all in terms of how they see or how they look at other black Africans from other parts of the continent. As one South African, Boitumelo Magolego, stated in the South African newspaper, the *Mail&Guardian*, in his May 2008 post in the column for Mandela Rhodes Scholars when the xenophobic terror against black African immigrants was going on:

"Makwerekwere is used to refer to black Africans who are not South Africans....

This word has a very negative sting to it and is often used with contempt....It has undertones which speak of how black Africans are believed to be sub–human, too dark and have a pungent smell.

Two other words also used in this regard are grigamba and kom–ver (as in the Afrikaans *kom van ver*) — each prepended with the relevant prefix (I- for singular and Ma- for plural, for example, in the case of grigamba: igrigamba and magrigamba).

Even though these words seem new to some people, I have been hearing them as far back as I can remember. My grandparents also say that these words have been in use for as long as they can remember.

What's my point? The contempt with which South Africans regard black African foreigners is not a post–democracy phenomenon....

I would like to address the ability to identify *makwerekwere* from a group of people.

Primarily *makwerekwere* are believed to have a black (as in coal black) skin complexion. They are believed to have a pungent smell.

It is said to be such a strong smell that I have heard a number of girls say that when walking by in a mall and it hits you, you cannot mistake it for anything but - (*makwerekwere!*).

I have been in a taxi where the passengers refused what was a Mozambican national entry into the taxi, retorting "*driver re na re ka se kgone*" (driver the assault on our nostrils is just too much to bear).

Lastly, there is language and accent (to identify a *makwerekwere*).

I have conversed on multiple occasions with people from Ghana, Benin, Nigeria, DRC, Uganda, Tanzania, Ethiopia, Kenya, Rwanda, Zimbabwe and Namibia, and I did not think nor notice that all those individuals had a particular smell.

I have been to Kenya and I did not think nor notice the people there to have had a particular smell (excuse the arrogance in proclaiming myself arbiter of who smells and who not).

Have I encountered this spoken of smell? Yes, I have (on multiple occasions). Do I think that all people from Africa are dark? No, I know many individuals from these countries who have a fair complexion. The Kenyan population, in general, I feel could pass off as "South African" - that is in terms of complexion.

Do I agree that there are some black foreigners who are a tad dark? Yes, but the same could be said for some South Africans."

So, there is deep contempt for black Africans from other African countries among many black South Africans. It's nothing new, and it's not going to stop. And it amounts to another form of apartheid – Black South Africa against the *rest* of Black Africa – to South Africa's detriment.

Such arrogance may have played a role in fuelling hostility towards the black immigrants but it's probably the misconception and wrong belief that the immigrants are responsible for the poverty and suffering of black South Africans, especially in the townships, which has been responsible for the xenophobic violence against black foreigners in South Africa more than anything else. Bigotry against blacks from other African countries has also played a role.

After the end of apartheid, black African immigrants in South Africa were now facing a new enemy, fellow Africans who did not want them there.

It may, indeed, be a new form of apartheid in a country that fought so hard, with the help of fellow Africans across the continent, to abolish this abominable institution.

Printed in the United States
146197LV00007B/27/P